Infallibility and Interpretation

by

R. J. Rushdoony
and
P. Andrew Sandlin

Chalcedon Foundation
Vallecito, California 95251

Printed on acid free paper.

Library of Congress Catalog Card Number:
ISBN 1-891375-11-3

Printed in the United States of America.

Published by Chalcedon Foundation
PO Box 158
Vallecito, CA 95251

Table of Contents

Section 1
By R. J. Rushdoony

Section 2
By P. Andrew Sandlin

Appendix 1
By P. Andrew Sandlin

Appendix 2
By P. Andrew Sandlin

Appendix 3
By P. Andrew Sandlin

This book is dedicated to the memory of Cornelius Van Til, whose ministry is timeless.

Infallibility and Interpretation

Section 1

by
R. J. Rushdoony

Chapter 1
The Doctrine of God and Infallibility

Scripture tells me that God, being God, is incapable of lying (*Num. 23:9*). Jesus Christ more explicitly defines Himself as the way, the truth, and the life (*Jn. 14:6*). There is no access to the Godhead except through Him. Scripture is explicit about identifying Jesus Christ with the Godhead, and God as *the truth*.

This doctrine of God is thus very important in the doctrine of Scripture. God cannot lie. He is also immutable, unchangeable. He is the same, yesterday, today, and forever. "For I am the LORD, I change not" (*Mal. 3:6*). Change means that things outside ourselves affect and govern our being. As creatures, we are dependent on a world of other peoples and a vast creation made by God. God has no such need for others nor a need for anything outside Himself. In fact, God expresses His displeasure with all double-minded men (*Jas. 1:6-7*).

There can be nothing prior to the one and eternal God so that there is nothing that can contribute to His being. He is forever one God in three Persons, and forever one, yet in three Persons. God Who cannot lie is thus forever *truth*, and all that He is and does is truth. *God therefore can speak only an infallible word*. In all other religions except those which have borrowed from or are imitative of the Bible, there is no doctrine of inerrancy nor infallibility. Bible religion, on the other hand, mandates it. The God Who speaks in and through the Bible speaks a necessarily infallible word. God is internally and eternally God, all wise and all perfect in all His being. His perfection is also a *moral* perfection, whereas in some religions this moral perfection is lacking, or is replaced by cleverness. Some native religions saw in their supreme being no moral excellence, but a constant cleverness that was a delight, rather than a moral strength.

Unless a religion arises after Christianity and is imitative of it, it has no doctrine of inerrancy nor infallibility because the question is essentially alien to it. On the other hand, in Christianity the doctrine of infallibility is an inescapable implication of its doctrines of God and revelation.

When we turn to the Bible, as against two works written as imitations thereof, the differences are many. Believers in the *Koran* and in the *Book of Mormon* are convinced of the truth and historicity of those works. They are given as true and historical. Much criticism has been leveled against both works, and we have no intention here of reporting on the history of this criticism.

Both the *Koran* and the *Book of Mormon* purport to be in continuity with the Bible, so they begin by making a claim to a final place in the history of revelation. The final truth in the history of revelation is in them, or will come through them. Islam left room for a great prophet yet to come, a king or *mahdi*, and Mormonism believes in a continuing revelation through the hands of the twelve apostles who rule the church. Thus, the finality of revelation is denied even as an arena of authoritative rule is set forth. The finality of the enscriptured Word is replaced with the finality of some men. In this step, a dramatic change in the faith has taken place, and a shift in authority. In the place of the infallible Word, we have the binding authority of a group of men. The new revelations undermine the Biblical one.

Orthodox theology thus speaks of the Bible's "verbal inspiration," "plenary inspiration," and so on. The Scriptures are the very words of God, the oracles of God. Van Til thus wrote, " . . . we may thus call this view of God and his relation to the world the *covenantal* view. As such it is exhaustively personal. There is no area in which man can find himself confronted with impersonal fact or law. All so-called impersonal laws and all so-called uninterpreted facts are what they are because they are expressive of the revelation of God's will and purpose."[1] This should tell us why the language of covenantalism is Reformed and Van Tilian. It is alien to antinomianism and holds to the personal and covenantal law of the Triune God.

Basic to Biblical Faith, to the Reformed Faith, is the belief in the sovereignty of God. The term *lord* is applied to

God in both Old and New Testaments and is in the Septuagint routinely rendered as *lord*, God, or sovereign. Calvinism has done justice to the doctrine of God's sovereignty and therefore has been most ready to champion inerrancy, because basic to that view of Scripture is God's lordship or sovereignty.

Where men reject God's sovereignty, they accept and exalt man's sovereignty, and man's reason then prevails over faith and God's sovereignty. Rationalism then too prevails over presuppositionalism, and theology is supplanted with humanistic calculations. We have then the world of the contemporary church, with God locked out by supposedly sovereign man.

The infallible God of Scripture can speak only an infallible word, and this He has done. No other word is possible from such a God. Humanism in its every form will require a god who cannot speak, or who speaks with a confused tongue. The God of Scripture is not such a God. He is *the Lord*, the Sovereign King over all creation. His word is the creating word, the infallible and inerrant word. In affirming the word of God as infallible, we affirm our faith that the God of Scripture is He Whom He says He is, and that we believe His every word, and by His grace, hope to live in terms of His every word.

---

1 C. Van Til, *The Doctrine of Scripture* (Den Dulk Foundation, 1967), 37.

Chapter 2

The Doctrine of God and of Scripture

The crisis of our time is a religious one with deep roots, although its immediate origin is in Charles Darwin and his theory of evolution. Some Victorians, like Matthew Arnold, saw the solution as the abandonment of religion, specifically Christianity, but the retention of morality, *i.e.*, the Victorian version of Biblical morality. Now we are in the midst of a revolution against Biblical law and morality, both within and outside of the church. Objections to teaching chastity in state schools are grounded on the premise that chastity is an anti-natural religious demand and, therefore, constitutes an establishment of religion. This is a valid claim.

As a result, state schools are teaching courses on self-chosen values of a purely humanistic character. Sexuality is held to be *natural* and the forms it takes matters of personal preference. Girls, at the onset of puberty, are taken by some parents to a doctor to be surgically deflowered and fitted for contraceptives. In some instances, parents encourage children to bring their sexual partner home and into their bedrooms for the night.

Contrary to Matthew Arnold's hopes, morality cannot stand in separation from religion, nor can any civilization long so endure.

Attempts to compromise Biblical Faith are not new. When the early church entered the intellectual world of the Greco-Roman Empire, the immediate efforts by the converts from paganism was to compromise and absorb the faith into existing culture, which was evolutionary. As a result, the true leading father of the Greek Orthodox Church became Plato, and of Rome, and later of Arminianism, Aristotle.

As a result, very early, many of these churchmen took a loose view of Genesis chapters 1-11. Some, like Gregory of Nyssa, held that all of the Mosaic books were symbolic; it was held that God could not be interested in things like dietary laws. History was thus eroded in favor of mythology, somewhat after the manner of Karl Barth.

At the heart of all this was an alien concept of God. For Greek philosophy, *idea*, or form, is ultimate, and *God* is a limiting concept posited to avoid an infinite regress in causality. Rather than a person, god was seen as *idea*, an abstraction, whereas the Biblical God is instead the Supreme *Being*, three persons with one *being*. For the Hellenic mind, the Biblical God is crude, and the Bible is crude, because it is totally personal and speaks of this Supreme Being as one capable of wrath, jealously, hatred, and love.

Thus, over the centuries, the theologians have commonly reflected this Greco-Roman view of God by viewing God as the supreme Idea, not as the Supreme Being and Person. One professor held, in a discussion, that the Biblical view of God was crude and demeaning to sound religion.

It is important for us to realize that the Biblical doctrine of God as the Supreme Being is basic to the doctrine of Scripture as the Word of God. The inerrancy of the Bible rests on it. Only the supreme and totally self-conscious God, Maker of heaven and earth and all things therein, can speak an infallible word. At the Council of Jerusalem, James declared, "Known unto God are all his works from the beginning of the world" (*Ac. 15:18*). Such knowledge is *total knowledge* that requires and rests on predestination. It also necessitates infallibility and inerrancy. The God possessing such total creative power and knowledge can *only* speak an infallible word. In fact, no other word is possible for Him. Because man's knowledge is limited and tentative, man can only speak a fallible and tentative word. Wherever the Bible replaces the church, reason, or any other thing as the source of truth, the doctrine of "scriptural inerrancy" immediately follows.

Implicit in various philosophies is a disguised form of infallibility, *i.e.*, reason, the scientific method, experience, and so on. Every system of thought has implicitly a doctrine of truth; however disguised with modest disclaimers, each rests on a bedrock of presuppositions which define and identify truth.

This doctrine of Scripture appears clearly in all the Bible. God's Word is the only certain word. It covers not only His enscriptured Word, but His actions as declared in that Word. God declares through Isaiah that His determination of history and His judgments are inescapable: "thou shalt know that I am the LORD" (*Is. 49:23, 26*). In Malachi 3:6, He declares, "I am the LORD; I change not." Whether in word, or in history, or in the realms of thought, God's Word is never a tentative word but always an infallible word.

This doctrine is perhaps the most revolutionary in all of history. There are no "holy" books in other religions unless they are imitative of the Bible, e.g., the Koran and the Book of Mormon. This fact alone has been revolutionary in history in that it has *mandated* literacy. Outside the world of Biblical Faith, literacy has been the province of experts, *i.e.*, scribes and the like. Pagan cultures could be highly advanced, with amazing skills in engineering, astronomy, architecture, and so on, but literacy was for most the specialized skill of a servant class. If, however, to know God means above all else to know His enscripturated Word, then literacy assumes a priority lacking in other cultures. It should not be surprising, therefore, that as Biblical Faith recedes, so too does literacy. Some educators now view many people as "non-literate" types who do not need literacy.

If one abandons belief in the inerrancy of the Bible, then belief in the God of Scripture is also discarded, to be replaced at best by an evolving god, or by a cosmic idea, or a goal of evolution as in Teilhard de Chardin. Any god falling short of the Biblical God cannot be man's savior. If He is not the absolute predestinating God, any salvation offered by such a god is a tentative one, not an eternal fact.

Added to that fact, we cannot truly *know* such a god. Instead of changing not, he changes, and salvation today can be damnation tomorrow. Instead of studying the Bible, we then must study nature to understand the next step in evolution. Like Aristotle, we shall look for freaks like a two-headed calf as possibly the next step in evolution. Or we can, like Emile Durkheim, view the criminal as an evolutionary pioneer, charting for us a new way of life in history. The evolutionary word replaces the certain, the infallible, Word of God.

Much is at stake, thus, in the doctrine of the infallible Word of God. Western civilization was once more or less Christian, whereas now it is basically humanistic and evolutionary. As a result, it is in growing collapse and paralysis and can only be revitalized by a systematically Christian faith.

The church too has gone over to the enemy. Very few seminaries hold now to the historicity of Genesis, chapters 1-11. Supposedly orthodox churches now treat candidates for the ministry who hold to the historicity of Genesis 1-11 with disrespect and suspicion. Having adopted another faith, they view with suspicion all who hold to the historical Faith.

As Richard Weaver said, "ideas have consequences," and false views of the Bible held within the church remake the world into an alien and man-centered realm. The world of accredited seminaries and colleges is rapidly becoming the world of militant anti-Christianity. The God of Scripture is being replaced by the god of Darwin and Chardin, a false god who does not know himself and therefore cannot know us.

More than one prominent pastor has in recent years down-graded attempts to revive the importance of the doctrine of infallibility by insisting that all that is necessary is that we hold to and preach John 3:16. But that verse loses all meaning if the doctrine of God and His Word are undermined. The validity of salvation rests on the doctrine of God and His certain Word. Remove that, and the abandonment of Christianity is underway. Those views of the Bible which deny its inerrancy lead step by step to an alien and false doctrine of God, to idolatry. Today, idolatry is all too prevalent in many churches.

Chapter 3

The Infallible Word

The Bible gives us a God Who, given the nature and being ascribed to Him, can only speak infallibly, inerrantly. It follows, given such a God, that we have *an infallible word*.

On the other hand, given the doctrine of man as a *fallible* creature, we have a very basic fact about man. Even in Eden, created without sin, he was potentially fallible. After the fall he is sinful, and after his regeneration, while fully capable of sin, his basic direction is obedience to God and His law-word. In eternity man is by God's grace forever beyond sinning.

Failure to understand what Thomas Boston called "the fourfold estate of man," and the eternal and perfect nature of God, leads to confusion. As the Enlightenment led to the erosion of theology, preaching began to exalt man rather than God. For some generations prior to World Wars I and II, popular theology was emphatic that man is immortal in his soul, this despite Paul's statement in 1 Timothy 6:16 that God "only hath immortality," and that man has the grace of resurrection. It is Jesus Christ who brings "life and immortality to light through the gospel" (*2 Tim. 1:10*). It is a gift of God, not an attribute.

Sinful man is at his best fallible and is thus not a valid source of knowledge, given this nature. Some years ago, as a youth, I heard an intelligent layman condemn theologians as apostate because the theologians he knew were rationalists. For him, this method denied the priority of God and supplanted God with the mind of man.

This is at the heart of the issue of inerrancy, of the battle between presuppositionalism and rationalism: whose word prevails, the Word of God, or the word of man? A man's answer to this question is a test of faith.

In the world of humanism, the word of man prevails. In many court cases involving Christian schools, home schools, church schools, and the like, the key question by state attorneys is very simply this: do you believe that the Bible is God's inerrant Word? To so believe is seen as a disqualification of learning or intelligence. The test is thus not one's knowledge or qualification, but one's religious presupposition. The question is who is truly God, truly ultimate, man or God, his Creator? To the humanist, good reasoning must presuppose the ultimacy of reason.

Isaiah warns us against this humanism: "Cease ye from man, whose breath is in his nostrils: for wherein is he to be accounted of?" (*Is. 2:22*). The worship of God requires that we know the absolute priority of God.

The Biblical doctrine of God is marked by a remarkable distinctive, namely, the radical association of God with truth. In Numbers 23:19 we are told that "God is not a man that he should lie." Titus 1:2 tells us that God cannot lie. Jesus Christ, God incarnate, states bluntly that there is no way to God other than the truth, and that He is the truth (*Jn. 14:6*). In brief, the Biblical doctrine of God so closely associates the truth with God that it asserts that God cannot lie because it is so alien to His being.

This means that Biblical Faith is radically truth-based, so much so that truth is cited as basic to the nature and being of God. Given this fact, we can understand why so close a relationship exists between Christianity and knowledge, between being and truth. The implications are enormous. Man is not alone in an uncharted cosmos but is in a realm created by God, Who is the truth, and which is knowable in terms of Him. Darwin's world is a dishonest realm because it presupposes by faith the reality of truth whereas his blind evolution should as readily vindicate a lie as anything. Darwin presupposes the reality of order, development, and consistency, of a total realm of truth which his theory does not make legitimate.

For Darwin, evolution must say, "I am the way, the truth, and the life," but it cannot do so. The cultural Christianity inherited by Darwin provides the framework for his hypothesis, a bad patchwork of borrowed ideas.

Darwin removes from the world of thought any objective standard or criterion for judgment so that the *infallible word* is replaced by *infallible evolution,* which lacks any valid criterion for judgment. One evolutionist, a professor, dismissed a student's questioning of evolution with the words, "It *cannot* be true." Evolution has become the great imitator of Christianity: it is now *the truth,* the way, and the life for mankind!

The issues at stake in any discussion of the infallible word are not trivial ones. The nature and being of God are at stake. To surrender the infallible word is to surrender Biblical Christianity and to replace it with another faith.

God does not today guide men directly and without the use of Scripture. The sufficiency of Scripture makes separate guidance unnecessary. The finality of Biblical revelation is an article of faith: it needs no supplemental revelations. The infallible word is also the sufficient word.

Jesus, in Matthew 5:17-20, affirms the absolute authority of every jot and tittle of the law of God. This is a very strong statement, and very important in affirming inerrancy. Not the slightest statement in the Mosaic Law can be overlooked. Its authority is total and its relevance is always limitless. We are not judges over God's Word but are judged by it.

Chapter 4

The Fallible God

As we have seen, law in every culture requires an exactitude because the life and death of men and society depends upon it. In present day court decisions, it is said that judgments have been based on the very punctuation of the text.

God's law is basic to His enscripturated Word, the Bible. Because God is the Creator of heaven and earth and all things therein, His law-word governs all things as they should be governed, accurately and fully. Inerrancy is a logical consequence of the Biblical doctrine of God.

Basic to theology is the doctrine of the *atonement*. No approach to God by fallen man is possible without it. The atonement removes the great gap between man and God, man's sin, and his lawlessness, his contempt for God's law in favor of his own. The substitute man offers for God's law is his own law; he replaces God's law-word with his own (*Gen. 3:1-6*). Law is made a human product, and man and the state replace God; the omnipotent state replaces the omnipotent God. Atonement becomes a merely ecclesiastical concern when law is reduced to a human product. Atonement, moreover, is reduced in meaning when it is separated from the fact of the *curse of sin* on the whole human race. Sin is much more than a problem man has; it is in his fall now inherent to his human nature so that he needs atonement, death, to rid himself of it, and regeneration, new life, to overcome it. The preaching of atonement without the fact of the curse and death is to warp and distort the doctrine.

Atonement tells us that the law is real and binding; atonement turns the law-breaker into a law-keeper because it is marked by a transformation of the sinner into a new creature in Christ. Man as he is, fallen man, hears no voice but his own. When he reads the Bible, he hears it at best as his own voice; he rejects the independence of God because it is the antithesis of his own claim to independence. He cannot tolerate inerrancy nor Biblical law because both doctrines threaten his own belief in his independence. Fallen man hears his own voice in everything, and the voice of God in nothing independent of himself. Apart from Reformed theology, we have only efforts that diminish God by exalting man.

At issue in the question of the inerrancy of Scripture is the question, "Whose voice shall we hear and obey?" It is either God's Word or man's word that is binding and determinative. Whenever and wherever we set aside the Word of God, we replace it with the word of man, whether we admit this fact or not.

B. B. Warfield very tellingly pointed out that, when the Bible speaks of the "prophetic word," it refers to itself. Men spoke from God, Peter tells us in 2 Peter 1:19-21. Warfield demonstrates that the writers of the Bible spoke from God. It was not their private interpretations they gave us, but the very words of God.[1] What Scripture says, God says. There is "an absolute identification, in the minds of these writers of Scripture with the speaking of God."[2] There is thus an identification of the Scriptures as the very word of God. Warfield summed up the Reformed doctrine of inspiration in these words:

> Inspiration is that extraordinary, supernatural influence (or passively, the result of it) exerted by the Holy Ghost on the writers of our Sacred Books, by which their words were rendered also the words of God, and therefore, perfectly infallible.[3]

The Westminster Confession of Faith, 1729, is the great Reformed statement on faith and doctrine — unlike most confessions, it *begins* with a long chapter on "Of the Holy Scriptures." The Bible is "the rule of faith and life" because it is the very Word of God. Chapter I, Section IV tells us that "The authority of the Holy Scripture, for which it ought to be believed and obeyed, dependeth not upon the testimony of any man or church, but wholly upon God (who is truth itself), the author thereof; and therefore it is to be receive, because it is the Word of God." We receive the

Bible as the Word of God by God's grace, not by our own wisdom, insight, or intelligence. Thus, the Bible does not depend on any church or scholar for verification. God alone provides it by His Spirit.

When we turn to Buddhism or Hinduism, we have no infallible nor unchanging word because they come from no such God, but only from men. There are hence many contradictory strains in such religions. The God of the Bible is unlike the gods of all other religions. He is omnipotent, omniscient, eternal, and totally self-conscious. There are no dark corners nor hidden, unconscious aspects to His being. He, therefore, speaks an infallible word and can *only* speak an infallible word. The doctrine of inerrancy was thus a necessary development of Biblical theology; any other view is alien to the Bible. The creeds of the church have from the beginning affirmed God to be the Creator of heaven and earth and all things therein, and the Savior of His appointed new humanity. The logic inherent in this faith has required the affirmation of the infallibility of Scriptures. We do not affirm a fallible God and therefore a fallible word. Those who deny the infallible word quickly follow this with a belief in the fallibility of God. They then have no assured salvation to offer, only a possible one.

---

[1] B. B. Warfield, *The Inspiration and Authority of Scripture* (Philadelphia, PA, 1948), 135f.

[2] *ibid.*

[3] *ibid.*, 420.

Chapter 5

Law and Inerrancy

Man's basic problem is not an *intellectual* but an *ethical* one, not mental but moral. The intellectual problems are the result of his moral ones. Man's fallen estate is a moral fall, not an intellectual one in its essence. The intellectual fall is due to his moral failure.

This is why the Bible gives us so different a religion; it is concerned, not with man's ignorance but man's sin. Man is ignorant because of his *moral* rejection of God.

The Bible, thus, does not offer us proof of God's *existence*; it presupposes that. What it does give us is God's *law* because it is God's law we have broken. We are *sinners, law-breakers*, who deny the Judge to evade His law and indictment.

The rejection of Christianity is a rejection of the God Who gave us His law and of the Christ Who alone can redeem us from the curse of the law. The Bible is the Word of that Triune God.

The Bible *presupposes* our *moral* blindness: hence God speaks. He has spoken "at sundry times and in diverse manners" (*Heb. 1:1*), and now "in these last days" by His Son, the Heir of all things and also their Creator (*Heb. 1:2*).

If we deny God's law, we deny the moral priority of the Word of God. The Bible then becomes for us something other than God's law-book. Instead of a *command* word, it becomes something else. But the Bible *is* God's word to man, a *command* word by the Creator-King to His *covenant* people.

The histories written by the scribes of the ancient world are untrustworthy; victories are overstated and defeats normally omitted. It is only *the laws* of antiquity which are accurately transmitted to us. Society cannot exist without laws because laws establish the necessary boundaries of life. To speak of *society* is to speak of a *community* or a communion. Hence, the *reliability* of the legal codes of the ancient world.

Because the Bible is the law of the kingdom of God, it not only states accurately the requirements of that kingdom, but it states them infallibly as well. If we deny to God His kingdom, we deny to Him His law. To deny either the law or the kingdom is to deny the other. They are inseparable.

In any discussion of Biblical infallibility it follows, therefore, that the law and its status are a relevant matter, and to deny to the law a perfect definition of God's justice is to deny to God His kingdom. Thus, antinomianism undermines the doctrine of Scripture and its infallibility. We have then only *history* left, in the main, yet an accurate history which lacks any moral criterion is no history at all. Quite logically, modernism has a *social gospel,* a gospel that desires morality for history from history, and which is a changing shifting word. Antinomianism has deadly consequences for the valid doctrine of Scripture.

Antinomianism denies to God, man, and history an objective and unchanging law and government. Its consequences are deadly for Biblical religion. To remove the law from Christianity is to remove it from the kingdom of God *and* from atonement, both of which presuppose law. Sin is the violation of or any lack of conformity to the law of God and if there is no law there is no sin, for 1 John 3:4 tell us that "sin is the transgression of the law."

The question of antinomianism is thus closely related to that of infallibility. The kingdom of God is a law-realm; entrance to it means atonement, the satisfaction of the law. To deny the law is to remove certainty with respect to salvation and the kingdom of God from Christianity.

To deny the law is to deny the kingdom of God and the Triune God. The doctrine of infallibility then is an abstract and a remote one.

We deal with law daily in all areas of life and thought. We are law-governed because we live in a particular realm. To remove law from that realm is to remove its life and meaning; it destroys all focus. The focus of Biblical law is the kingdom of God and His righteousness (*Mt. 6:31*). As a result of modern antinomianism, the focus of the church has been on *personal* salvation, as with Arminianism, or *social* salvation, as with modernism. If there is no law, there is no kingdom.

There is then no sound focus for life. I was told some years ago of a very able man, who, having no faith nor focus for living, read the "personal" and related want ads in the daily newspaper. He lived vicariously in the strange world of lonely people, himself more and more isolated to unreality.

Today churchmen who have separated themselves from a valid doctrine of the Bible and of God are likewise more and more irrelevant to God and His creation because they have separated themselves from truth and reality.

For unbelievers, the doctrines of God and of Scripture are seemingly difficult and peripheral ones, when in reality it is in doubt that man has separated himself from reality. We must believe in order that we may understand.

Chapter 6

The Bible and Meredith G. Kline

The interpretation of the Bible has too often been determined by the cultural context of the church. In the Greco-Roman world, the Bible, while exerting great power, was too often interpreted in terms of alien ideas. In the world of the Orthodox churches, Plato's influence was strong; later, in the Western churches, Aristotle became the major extraneous influence.

With John Calvin, Biblical premises predominated, but, in time, these gave way to other veins, at first Arminian and thereafter neo-Thomistic, and then "scientific," especially after Charles Darwin. As a result, there is a renewed paganization of the church underway.

An interesting and important example of the importation of alien premises is Meredith G. Kline. In the May, 1958 *Westminster Theological Journal*, in a study entitled "Because It Had Not Rained" (Vol. XX, Nov. 1957, 133-157), Kline cast doubt on the Genesis 1 account of creation. The article raised questions and protests, but Kline assured Cornelius Van Til that he believed in the historicity of the Genesis account. However, some years later, writing on "Space and Time in the Genesis Cosmogony" in *The American Scientific Journal* (48:2-15, 1996), Kline made it clear that he did not see Genesis 1 as historical.

In *Kingdom Prologue* (Vol.1, 1981), Kline made clear his adherence to symbolic theology. Meanwhile, his influence in some 40 years on numerous seminary students has been a considerable one. It is very important, therefore, to see what Kline has to say. There are some major departures from the historic Faith. In *The Treaty of the Great King, The Covenant Structure of Deuteronomy: Studies and Commentary* (1963), Kline's perspective is a form of dispensationalism in that God's law is seen as valid only for the Hebrew commonwealth. Since a covenant with God is a treaty of law given by grace to His creation, the covenant idea is invalidated. Since love is the fulfilling of the law, the covenant cannot be reduced to love without law. Love is the *fulfilling,* putting into force, of the law. Any other interpretation does violence to Matthew 5:17.

In *Kingdom Prologue,* Kline uses symbols like a modern Swedenborg and sees correspondences where, at best, they are remote and not essential. The creation of man is described with all kinds of correlations to marriage, so that we are given a vague sense of mystical mysteries which only Kline can penetrate. (A student who has followed Kline in these views is James Jordan.)

It is Kline's article on "Space and Time in the Genesis Cosmogony" that best reveals his position. Genesis is for Kline a "two-register" view of Scripture, one "figurative," the other "literal." We are now in the world of Karl Barth's mundane history on the one hand, and holy history, on the other. Holy history is not lived within the natural order. The heavenly level is the upper register and the earthly level is the lower, historical register. This for Kline is the correct way to interpret the Bible. Genesis 1 is upper register "history."

This summary of Kline's views at once makes clear some important aspects of his view of the Bible. *First* of all, it spells the death of Protestantism to a startling degree. Of the countless millions who have read the Bible, how many have read what Kline says it means? John Tyndale, in translating the Bible into English, used an English old fashioned in his day because it was simpler and more basic. His hope was for every English plowboy to read and understand it. He did not finish his work before his execution, but nine-tenths of the Authorized Version (the King James) is his work.

In Kline's view, the Bible is known only by experts like himself. What plowboy will understand Kline? For that matter, not all scholars do. Kline's is an elitist view that militates against the very life of the Faith — given his perspective, Protestantism and the Reformed faith must be discarded.

Second, in reading Scripture as simple believers, we become disciples of Jesus Christ. In reading it *a la* Kline, we become disciples of Kline. In the histories of heresy, we see men becoming disciples of a man, not of the Lord, members of a sect, not of the kingdom. His is a novel view, not a restoration of abandoned premises.

Third, the Bible in his view becomes a subject of eisegesis, exotic interpretations which stress an individual's novel views. Cornelius Van Til made clear that only two views are possible, autonomy, self-law, or theonomy, God's law. Kline's view leads to an erosion of exegesis, so that strange and novel meanings appear among some of his followers. The naïve believer is viewed with scorn and contempt as lacking the level of intelligence to understand the Bible correctly. Such arrogance is neither faith nor grace. As one Kline disciple said, "Not knowing the Hebrew, you cannot grasp the meaning." But many who know the Hebrew simply cannot accept Kline's views.

Fourth, with the rise of critical views of the Bible, the office of elder has declined because the Bible is reduced to a book for experts. But the translation of the Bible into the languages of countless peoples has only increased the knowledge of the Faith. Where the Bible is the expert's domain, the Faith is markedly weaker. Moreover, those who see the Bible as their province because they are the experts seem to be lacking in the marks of faith, beginning with humility and grace. Kline certainly has created his own scholarly jargon.

Acquaintance in my youth with a few Scottish elders made me aware of their theological and Biblical knowledge. More than a few American elders were deeply versed in Biblical knowledge. The notable oilman, J. Howard Pew, in a discussion at his winter residence in Arizona some years ago cited to me whole chapters of the *Westminster Confession of Faith* from memory. Not only had he memorized the Shorter Catechism, but all of the Confession, and he had an excellent understanding of it. His problem was that, having grown up in simpler and more Christian America, he had trouble recognizing original sin in the clergy. He believed erring clergy were misguided rather than evil.

Today such informed elders and laymen are more uncommon. Biblical scholars often express contempt for trusting believers. The words "fundamentalist" and "Calvinist" are used by them to show disrespect for those who take the Bible at face value. Kline is not exempt from this.

Such scholars have made the Bible, in effect, a closed book to believers who are guided by the Bible rather than by scholars. Such arrogance is the negation of the meaning and intent of the Bible.

Is it not the case then, that Kline is expressing his contempt for God except as Kline himself can edit, correct, and interpret Him? Where is the Word of God in such views? A great deal is at stake in the compromising views of the Bible that are increasingly in evidence among evangelical and Reformed seminary professors. Can such views be tolerated without blasphemy, or can they rest without judgment?

Turning again to Kline's study of "Space and Time in the Genesis Cosmogony," we find that Kline, in Note 3 says, "Theological differences aside, the cosmology of mythology is analogous. Indeed, mythology may be defined formally precisely as a portrayal of human affairs in terms of a dynamic interrelating of divine and human affairs." Clearly, like many of the Barthians and related schools, he gives more weight to mythology than to Biblical history. Of course, a mythological view gives freedom to a scholar's view of Genesis 1, whereas a literal view lends them no such opportunity. Kline, in Note 47, says, "In this article, I have advocated an interpretation of Biblical cosmogony according to which Scripture is open to the current scientific view of a very old universe and, in that respect, does not discountenance the theory of the evolutionary origin of man. But while I regard the widespread insistence on a young earth to be deplorable disservice to the cause of biblical faith, I at the same time deem commitment to the cause of Scriptural teaching to involve the acceptance of Adam as an historical individual, the covenant head and ancestral fount of the rest of mankind, and the recognition that it was the one and the same divine act that constituted him the first man, Adam the son of God (*Luke 3:38*), that also imparted to him life (*Gen. 2:7*)." What happened? Evolution is true, according to Kline, and so is Adam historical. Did God at some point tap a primate and call him Adam? Such compromises always end up in absurdities. Kline's view of Genesis is clearly defective and dangerous to the church.

Chapter 7

Van Til's View

Over the centuries, the great Christian theologians have insisted that the Word of God posits the sovereign, omnipotent, and Triune God and, at the same time, that this God requires a doctrine of inerrancy. The two doctrines go hand in hand; the one requires the other.

This is very clearly seen in the various writings of Cornelius Van Til. This is especially true of his long, sixty-five page "Introduction" to B. B. Warfield's *The Inspiration and Authority of the Bible* (Philadelphia, PA, 1948).

Van Til began by insisting on the inseparability of facts and interpretation. All factuality as we know it is interpreted factuality. The results may be true or false, but facts and interpretation are inseparable. Thus, the facts we know are always interpreted facts. Now this relationship between facts and theory can lead us to some varying conclusions, and some have taken the idea that we do not see the facts in and of themselves but in the light of our personal categories of thought as a premise for a new kind of modernism. It has strengthened the phenomenalism which began essentially with Immanuel Kant. Every school of thought, faced with this character of facts and ideas, goes astray unless they begin with the self-contained God of Scripture. The God of Scripture, whose sovereign decree and plan embrace all things, is the place wherein facts and interpretations take place, and their context. Prior to all facts and interpretations is God and His sovereign decree and purpose. To begin with anything else is to begin with, for example, reason, and to reduce God to a finite status. All such alternate systems and theologies, whether of Aquinas or Butler, have reduced God to a finite god or an idol. Such systems also give us a man who is his own god and is himself the creative discoverer of truth. From the Biblical perspective, such a man is a sinner and a covenant-breaker.

It is thus an issue between sovereign man or sovereign God as to who is the true interpreter, God through His Word, or man by his word:

> If God is really self-contained and if he has really causally created this world and if he really controls it by his providence then the revelation of himself and about this world must be that of fully *interpreted fact*. All facts in the whole of created reality are then God-interpreted.[1]

This is true of nature no less than the Bible and its history. Man as a sinner wants to suppress the truth about God and His revelation. We are limited, fallen creatures, incapable of knowing the fullness of God and His handiworks, so "only God can reveal God."[2]

Because the God of Scripture is He Who made all things by His sovereign will and decree, He alone controls all things. The creature's will is at best a secondary and created power. It cannot will or decree the present nor the future apart from God's ordination and decree. God's will, not man's, is the final point of reference. The fact of a sovereign God Who is Creator and Lord over all makes knowledge possible because it abolishes chance and ensures the absolute determination of all things.

As with John Calvin, as with Van Til, knowledge is possible because chance has been abolished from creation. We have an infallible Word that speaks with clarity and knowledge about not only salvation but also as to the nature of reality. All things are God-created and, therefore, all things are knowable. There are no dark corners in God's universe, unknowable to Him and unexplorable. All things are His handiwork. If chance be admitted into creation, then knowledge becomes impossible. We know because God's creation can be known.

Thus, the doctrine of the Bible's infallibility is important to *every* sphere of knowledge because it declares that God the Creator is our source of knowledge. Things can be known because they are God-created. They are not brute factuality, but God-created facts. Their existence and their meaning are thus inseparable. To assume a world of brute or meaningless factuality is to deny the possibility of knowledge.

A strictly Buddhist science is impossible, because for Buddhism all things are illusion and without meaning. Modern thought, with its anti-Christianity, is essentially dishonest because it assumes a semi-Buddhist cosmos while at the same time operating on the very Christian theistic presuppositions it denies. Knowledge is possible because the universe is what the Bible says it is. It is God-created and it is a *universe*, not a multiverse; it is one common realm of meaning established by the Creator, the Triune God. It is this Christian worldview that makes knowledge possible. It makes possible certain knowledge and an assured faith.

Our problem today is that ostensibly Christian thinkers refuse to challenge the world of unbelief by challenging its epistemology, its theory of knowledge. Having retreated from this basic issue and battle, such men continue their retreat. They surrender the orthodox doctrine of Scripture for a false one, and they then logically continue their retreat because they have surrendered the interrelated doctrines of infallibility and the Triune Creator God Who is the only source of meaning and truth.

More is involved in the doctrine of Scripture than the important doctrine of six-day creationism, the atonement, the incarnation, and more. At stake is the Christian Faith and more. It is valid knowledge about God and about the world, about ourselves and history, about all things. Apart from this starting point, the surrender of knowledge becomes more and more extensive.

---

[1] Cornelius Van Til, "Introduction," in B. B. Warfield, *The Inspiration and Authority of the Bible* (Philadelphia, PA, 1948), 29f.

[2] *ibid.*, 35.

Infallibility and Interpretation

Section 2

by
P. Andrew Sandlin

Introduction

The following chapters are not so much a slim introduction to the art of Biblical interpretation (called "hermeneutics" these days), but rather a discussion of the conditions under which interpretation is possible at all. The Rev. Steve Schlissel, noted Reformed pastor, once shrewdly stated, "We do not begin by exegeting the Bible, but by exegeting our presuppositions." Mine is a section about exegeting presuppositions.

Many fine works provide helpful advice about the procedure for interpreting the Bible. I cannot adequately add to these works. Even the best of them, however, are usually tainted by Enlightenment premises. They do not, for example, see interpretation as a theologically, historically, and socially shaped activity. This is especially true of evangelical views of interpretation, which really are carrying on the nineteenth-century liberal tradition at this point. They are naive "objectivists" who think they come to the Bible in a vacuum. They do not grasp that, in a very real sense, we get out of the Bible what we bring to it.

It is only fair that I alert readers to my own theological presuppositions. I am distinctly Reformed in my theology, though I value the contribution of all other sectors of orthodox Christianity. I have a deep regard for the history of Biblical interpretation. As the reader will soon detect, I hold that all these presuppositions guide — *must* guide — the interpretive task.

My own ministry is to get people to look at, detect, and acknowledge their own often hidden presuppositions. It is only then that they are in a position to positively address the issues that confront them.

I am grateful to Susan Burns for her work of typing and proofreading, as well as Walter Lindsay for proofreading. As always, I am thankful to Chalcedon for giving me the time to research and write.

Finally, it is a privilege to collaborate with Rousas John Rushdoony in this work. Aside from my godly parents, no one has had a more profound influence on my thinking. He truly is — and always will be — my theological mentor.

Chapter 1

The Foundation of Biblical Interpretation

All scripture is given by inspiration of God, and is profitable for doctrine, for reproof, for correction, for instruction in righteousness: That the man of God may be perfect, throughly furnished unto all good works.

2 Timothy 3:16, 17

2 Timothy 3:16 and 17 is the *locus classicus* (classic location) of the doctrine of the verbal inspiration of the Bible.[1] But it is more than that. It is also the *locus classicus* of the doctrine of the *Biblical interpretation* of the Bible. This is not designed to be a cute turn of phrase. It is an anchor of our Faith. St. Paul assures Timothy that the divinely inspired Scriptures taught him from his youth and which he now possesses completely furnish the man of God in his work. That is, the Bible fully equips him in his ministerial task. For Paul, it is the Holy Scriptures (and he was referring specifically to the Old Testament) that equip the man of God in his task of preaching, teaching, exhorting, discipling, and in general advancing the cause of Jesus Christ in the earth.

It is hard to imagine, however, that if the Bible fully equips the man of God, the key to understanding the Bible is to be found somewhere else. If that were the case, the Word of God would not *fully* equip the man of God. There is no key to be found somewhere else for unlocking the meaning of the Bible; the key is within the text of the Bible itself. This is to say that *the Bible is the source of its own interpretation.*[2] Properly understood, this means that the Bible is *self-interpreting*.

If Paul's exhortation to Timothy (and other teachings in the Bible) does not imply this proposition, then it will be difficult to explain how the Bible can fully equip the man of God in his calling. If the key to understanding the Bible is something or someone other than the Bible, then the Bible cannot fully equip the man of God. It is actually some other person, institution, book, or teaching that must equip the man of God. But this leads to an infinite regress. For what key will then help us to understand *this* particular key which helps us to understand the Bible? If someone or something other than the Bible constitutes the key for interpreting the Bible, what is the key to interpret that something or someone that constitutes the key to interpreting the Bible? For instance, if church tradition or some pastor or Pope is really the key to Biblical interpretation, what is the key to the interpretation of the tradition, pastor, or Pope? We discover that once we transfer the *locus* of the interpretation of the Bible from the Bible itself to something or someone else, we fall into a bottomless interpretive abyss. Holding that the Bible is the source of its own interpretation does not solve all theological problems, but at least it limits them to our understanding of a single Book.

Revelation and Interpretation

The inspired, infallible Word of the living God comes to us in exclusively oracular form. It confronts us in words, sentences, and books — in short, a written, propositional revelation of the voice of the Triune God.[3] This is why proper Biblical interpretation is so important; if we misinterpret the Scriptures, we misunderstand God's revelation to us. When we grasp this crucial point, we understand that *revelation and interpretation are inextricably bound to each other*. For if we misinterpret the Bible, it is no longer revelation that confronts us, but rather our own twisted misunderstanding of the revelation which we nonetheless consider revelation. In other words, we assume we are holding a divinely authoritative revelation when what we are really holding is a distortion — sometimes a dangerous distortion — of that revelation.

Now, notice I just said we interpret the Bible. But I said a moment ago that the Bible is self-interpreting. Is this self-contradictory? No, for I am using the word *interpret* in two different senses. When I say that the Bible is self-interpreting, I mean that it requires no *external* key to interpret it. But when I say *we* must interpret the Bible, I simply mean that we must necessarily construe what its words and message mean. There is, in fact, no such thing as uninterpreted revelation. Every time we read the Bible at home, every time we hear it preached in church, every time we see or hear it quoted in speech or writing, we necessarily interpret it.[4] To say that the issue of Biblical interpretation is not important is to say that it is not important to understand what God meant by what He wrote in the Bible. Therefore, anyone who does not take the issue of Biblical interpretation seriously does not take the Word of God seriously. The fact that the Bible is the sole source of its interpretation, therefore, is just as important as the fact that it is the sole source of God's revelation. If we misinterpret it, it is no longer a revelation, but a dilution, misunderstanding, or perversion of revelation.

Ecclesiastical Interpretation

It has not always been recognized that the Bible is the exclusive source of its own interpretation. In the medieval West, for example, the Roman Catholic Church devised the view that "tradition," and, more specifically, the institutional church as the guardian of that tradition, is the supreme interpreter of Sacred Scripture.[5] This notion enjoyed a certain acceptance in the patristic church (about A. D. 100-500), which often recognized the apostolic testimony both written and unwritten as divinely authoritative.[6] I should hastily point out, however, that the patristic fathers were not interested in a traditional or ecclesiastical understanding of the Bible *coordinate with but apart from* the Old and New Testament themselves. In the New Testament and patristic era, the Old Testament was regarded as God's exclusive inscripturated authority, to which was added, of course, the teachings of Christ and His apostles that later comprised the New Testament canon. These latter were set on a par with the infallible authority of the Old Testament.[7] It would never have occurred to the New Testament apostles and teachers, nor to the patristic fathers, to posit church authority as a separate key to Biblical interpretation. Biblical interpretation they indeed considered the task of the church, but that interpretation was simply what Christ and the apostles had taught and handed down.[8]

Increasingly, however, in both East and West, the source of Biblical interpretation was shifted from the apostles and Christ to the institutional church itself as expressed in its hierarchy. The rationale for this shift is possible only on the assumption that the institutional church itself retains lineal apostolic authority. That is, the church preserves apostolic authority in its own living tradition. After all, if Christ and His apostles are the exclusive source of Biblical interpretation, the church must retain apostolic stature if it is to legitimately adopt the role of Biblical interpreter. This is precisely what the Roman Church did.[9] In effect, the church held that it perpetuated the apostolic age as far as the matter of authority is concerned.

But we must go one step further. The apostles were charged not merely with interpreting the Word; some of them were divinely charged with speaking that word under direct, divine inspiration. Therefore, it was natural for the Roman Church eventually to set its own pronouncements on a par with canonical Scripture. The Council of Trent, convened to counter the successes of those pesky, Bible-thumping Protestants, posited unwritten tradition *and* the Biblical canon as coordinate authorities.[10] Later, after discovering it was not sufficient to set unwritten ecclesiastical tradition on a par with Scripture — since it was necessary eventually to specify exactly how that tradition was infallibly communicated — the church decreed the infallibility of the Pope when he speaks in his papal office, *ex cathedra* (1869-1870). The regression is easily discernible: what began as an attempt to furnish an ecclesiastical key to Biblical interpretation apart from the Bible degenerated into the assumption of Jesus Christ and His "vicar" on earth as *coordinate* authorities. *The denial of the Bible as the exclusive source of its interpretation eventually leads to the denial of the Bible as the exclusive source of divine revelation.*

Individualistic Interpretation

Another competing claimant to the source of Biblical interpretation is man as an individual — his reason, experience, or intuition. This view is less sophisticated, though perhaps more dangerous, than that of the Roman Catholic Church. This is the class of modern existential Christians (both Protestant and Roman Catholic) who hold *man as an individual* as the source of Biblical interpretation. This is exhibited most notably among many modern charismatics.[11] We should distinguish between the claims, on the one hand, of one's getting new prophetic revelations on a par with the Bible, and on the other, on one's getting individualistic illumination about the Bible's interpretation. We may see the first as obviously erroneous,[12] but the second is no less mistaken. It is exhibited in statements like, "Dear, what did the Holy Spirit say to *you* in that Bible verse?" The meaning of Scripture thereby is identified with what one considers the Spirit's revelation to the individual. Make no mistake: God does indeed illuminate to our eyes the meaning of Scripture (*Ps. 119:18*), but what the Spirit illuminates is the objective, verifiable revelation. In simple terms, the statements of the Bible do not have one meaning for one man, church, or organization, and another meaning for another man, church, or organization. In interpreting the Bible, the variable does not exist in the meaning of Scripture, but only in the mind of (sinful) man. This is why there are differing, conflicting interpretations, not because God in the Bible says different things to different people.

To those Christians who do not grasp this point, the Bible is no longer the source of its own interpretation; rather, the mind of man (falsely equated with the Holy Spirit's leading) is considered the source of its interpretation. This is materially no different from the Roman Catholic notion of tradition as the source of the Bible's interpretation.

Some Christians, properly recognizing the errors mentioned above, nonetheless embrace another form of individualistic interpretation. They completely shut out other believers, both past and contemporary, in the interpretative task. They are right to resist Rome's sectarian, ecclesiastical interpretation of Scripture. They are right to argue that God has given every Christian the solemn obligation and privilege of scriptural interpretation. But they are wrong to suggest that God gave this obligation and privilege to each believer *apart from* every other believer. God opens up the meaning of the Bible to other Christians besides us! To say we rely on the Holy Spirit alone to help us understand the Bible while not inquiring about how the Spirit leads (or led) other reverent Christians to interpret it is an arrogance of the greatest magnitude. Pinnock notes:

> There is something audacious about such a leap from the twentieth century back into the first century without even a glance at the ways in which Scripture has hitherto been understood. Indeed, in such a case there is the real danger that the interpreter will bring the Bible under his own control. *Every explicit denial of tradition involves a hidden commitment to a personal brand of tradition.* We cannot stand apart from the spirit of the age and time altogether, but we stand in need of the chastening of two millennia of biblical study.[13]

This approach avoids the pitfalls at either side of the correct interpretive road.[14] First, it opposes the *coordinate* authority of the Bible and church tradition as it stands in Eastern Orthodoxy[15] and Rome. This confounds the Word of God and the word of man. Second, the correct approach combats the individualism that denies the Holy Spirit's leadership in the lives of other Christians and the catholic (universal) church historic, a view that dominates much of modern evangelical Christianity.[16] We must insist that no church or its hierarchy may arrogate to itself the exclusive right to interpret the Bible, but we must equally insist that no individual Christian may do this. We need the contribution of our brothers in interpreting the Bible.

The Valid Role of Teachers

To assert that the Bible is the exclusive source of its own interpretation, in fact, demands the role of pastors, teachers, Biblical and interpretive helps, and so forth. To abandon them would be a serious error. Why? Because they are *aids* in the interpretative task. Here is the key: Biblically reverent pastors, scholars, teachers, and their writings are not the source of interpretation; they help us to better understand the Bible as the source of its *own* interpretation. To assert that the Bible is the exclusive source of its interpretation is not to say that the Bible requires no human interpretation. If the Bible were self-interpreting *in the sense that* men need only read it and immediately grasp its meaning, we would not need to study it and mine its vast revelational riches. Its meaning would in all cases be self-evident, and there would be no dispute about it. But, as anyone knows, this is simply not the case. As noted earlier, when anybody reads or hears the Bible, he interprets it. *Interpretation is an inescapable concept.* The question is not whether we will interpret the Bible, but where we will go to discover what that interpretation should be. And the answer to the last question is simply, the Bible. This is why lexicons, commentaries, systematic theologies, pastors, scholars, teachers, and so forth are required. They are not the source of the Bible's interpretation; *they are the source of helpful information about the Bible's interpretation.* Those evangelicals and others who claim, "I never read any books or commentaries since they are written by men; I only read the Bible," are not merely foolish; they are arrogant. They are quite correct to recognize that the Bible is the source of its own interpretation, but they are quite wrong to assume that they never need human assistance in grasping the Bible's interpretation. I repeat: the role of these human aids is not to interpret the Bible for us but to help us understand how the Bible should be interpreted. There is a significant difference here. Unlike the Roman Catholic and Eastern Orthodox view, the church and its pastors and teachers are not sources of interpretation; Biblically, they are merely sources of information *about* interpretation. In simple terms, if understanding the meaning of the Bible's message is crucial, we can use all the help we can get in understanding it.

In summary, the Bible is not only God's verbally inspired and infallible revelation; it is also the source of its interpretation. Neither ecclesiastical tradition nor individualist subjectivism is the source of the Bible's interpretation. Nonetheless, God graciously provides pastors, teachers, scholars, and their writings to help us gain a greater knowledge of the Bible so that we can interpret it properly.

---

1 Few have expressed its significance more succinctly but powerfully than John Calvin: "This is a principle which distinguishes our religion from all others that we know that God hath spoken to us, and are fully convinced that the prophets did not speak at their own suggestion, but that, being organs of the Holy Spirit, they only uttered what they had been commissioned by heaven to declare," *Commentaries on the Epistles to Timothy, Titus, and Philemon*, in *Calvin's Commentaries* (Grand Rapids, 1993), 21:248-249.

2 Gerhard Ebeling, *The Word of God and Tradition* (Philadelphia, 1968), 127.

3 Carl F. H. Henry, *God, Revelation and Authority* (Waco, TX, 1979), 3:455-481, and William J. Martin, "Special Revelation as Objective," in ed., Carl F. H. Henry, *Revelation and the Bible* (Grand Rapids, 1958), 61-72.

4 Gerhard Ebeling, *The Problem of Historicity* (Philadelphia, 1967), 9-33.

5 Yves Congar, *The Meaning of Tradition* (New York, 1964).

6 J. N. D. Kelly, *Early Christian Doctrines* (New York, 1960 edition), 33.

7 *ibid.*, 31-32.

8 Jaroslav Pelikan, *The Emergence of the Catholic Tradition* (Chicago and London, 1971), 109-120.

9 *idem.*, *The Riddle of Roman Catholicism* (New York and Nashville, 1959), 26.

10 Philip Schaff, *The Creeds of Christendom* (Grand Rapids [1931], 1990), 2:80.

11 Ian Cotton, *The Hallelujah Revolution* (Amherst, NY, 1996). They appeared in the patristic church: Ronald A. Kydd, *Charismatic Gifts in the Early Church* (Peabody, MA, 1984), 31-36.

12 Kenneth L. Gentry, Jr., *The Charismatic Gift of Prophecy* (Memphis, 1989 edition).

13 Clark H. Pinnock, *Biblical Revelation* (Chicago, 1971), 118-119, emphasis supplied.

14 It is the historic Protestant view: Alister McGrath, *Reformation Thought* (Oxford, 1993 edition), 144-147.

15 On the Eastern Orthodox view of the relation between Scripture and tradition, see John Meyendorff, *Byzantine Theology* (New York, 1974, 1979), 4-11.

16 Robert E. Webber, *Common Roots* (Grand Rapids, 1978), 14-16. See also Andrew Sandlin, "Protestantism vs. Primitivism," in ed., Sandlin, *Keeping Our Sacred Trust* (Vallecito, CA, 1999), 55-81.

Chapter 2

Biblical Infallibility and Biblical Interpretation

When we say that the Bible is the infallible Word of God, we are not making a statement merely about *formal* Biblical authority. We are equally making a statement about *material* Biblical authority.[1] We are not, in other words, offering merely a description of the Bible's level of accuracy, which *formal* Biblical authority does. In addition, we are making a statement about the *nature* of the God Who inspired the Bible, the type of book the Bible is, and what the Bible actually teaches; this is *material* Biblical authority. We must be careful to recognize that the doctrine of infallibility does not arise from an inductive reading of certain isolated texts.[2] If that were the case, we would have to answer why we should accept those texts as divinely inspired in the first place. This is a supreme error of evidentialist apologetics for the Bible. A prime example is the late John Gerstner, an outstanding Reformed theologian, who wished initially to establish the general historical reliability of the gospels and only *subsequently* to consult these teachers of doctrine to see what they have to say about the infallibility of the Bible.[3] This has things just backwards. Fundamentally, the Bible is not infallible because its writers say so; they say so, because as the living Word of God, it can be nothing *but* infallible. We affirm the infallibility of the Word of God because the God Whom we serve can utter no other word besides an infallible Word (*Jn. 17:17; Titus 1:2*). It is not hard to detect, therefore, how the doctrine of Biblical infallibility is bound up inextricably with the doctrine of God and the theology of the Bible's own interpretation. The grave error in Gerstner's approach is that it cannot give a sufficient reason why we should accept the Bible as generally accurate historically if the God Whom it posits and reveals is not Who He says He is, or if, worse yet, if He does not exist. We need the God Whom the Bible reveals as the absolute source of Biblical inspiration and infallibility: it does no good to speak of "general historical reliability" unless we presuppose the God Whose providence can assure that these inspired records are historically reliable.[4]

Subverting Infallibility While Affirming It

When we do not understand or if we eliminate the truth that Biblical infallibility is as much a statement about formal Biblical authority as it is material Biblical authority (as we defined them above), we will likely fall into serious predicaments and end up subverting the authority of the Bible. We leave ourselves vulnerable to certain interpretative methods that may undermine the infallibility of the Bible, all the while claiming to affirm Biblical infallibility. The most notable example in recent history is the theological system known as dispensationalism.[5] Dispensationalists almost to a man affirm Biblical infallibility, and they are often at the forefront of the defense of this viewpoint. That their theological suppositions dismiss the relevance of large portions of the Bible belies their affirmation of Biblical infallibility. What good does it do to say that the Bible is without error if we equally argue that about three fourths of it has no binding authority today, and has had no binding authority for nearly two thousand years? Technically a textbook on geometry may be infallible, but it is not *that* infallibility for which we Christians should stand. The assertion of infallibility is equally an assertion of Biblical *authority*. Dispensational theology creates a particular interpretative scheme that invalidates its claims of Biblical infallibility.

The same is true of some ostensibly within the Reformed camp. One thinks immediately of scholars like Meredith Kline, whose assault on the literal creation account in Genesis 1 and 2 includes the explicit admission that his tack assures the scientist need not bother about Biblical constraints in his investigation of the origins of man and the universe.[6] To say that this idea is compatible with the infallibility of Scripture is to talk nonsense. The truth of Genesis 1 and 2 impinges quite directly on a topic some modern scientists investigate — the origin of the universe — and therefore it surely "constrains" scientists who wish to arrive at the *truth* about origins. If we affirm Biblical infallibility but deny the right of the Bible to speak authoritatively on certain subjects on which it quite obviously does speak, we have denied its infallibility, no matter what our assertion may be.

Dispensationalists wipe out their claims for Biblical infallibility by canceling the authority of much of its revelation. Kline undermines any consistent assertions of Biblical infallibility by applying extra-Biblical literary standards to the Bible which render its actual literary structure meaningless — not to mention that it may sever the Christian message from its being anchored in human history. Whatever this is, it is *not* Biblical infallibility.

Infallibility and Authority

Significantly, our Reformed forebears did not argue for such an abstract idea of infallibility. For them, the Bible's infallibility was a corollary of its majesty — the Bible is infallible because it is the very Word of the living God Who can speak in no other way than infallibly.[7] For this reason, they were not often given to excessive harmonization. That is, they did not usually try hard to reconcile statements of the Bible that on the surface *seemed* to contradict. Their high reverence for God's majesty persuaded them that the Bible is true, even when it *seemed* to contradict itself. In Van Til's view, if God is Who He said He is (the omnipotent, all-controlling Sovereign), and if we are who He says we are (finite, wholly contingent creatures made in His image), we can expect seeming — though no actual — contradictions in the Bible.[8] The inspiration and infallibility of the Bible are mysteries no less than the Trinity and the two natures of Christ. We do not understand precisely how the Bible is infallible, nor how it can be both the Word of God and the word of man; and it is not our job to *demonstrate* its infallibility. Biblical infallibility, like every other doctrine, is fundamentally a matter of faith, not of demonstration.

Infallibility and Exegesis

God, Who Himself is truth (*Jn. 14:6, 9-10*), speaks nothing but truth. Because the Scripture in exhaustive degree is His Word, when we read it and interpret it, we know that we are reading and interpreting the infallible message of God. This relieves the so-called tension between Biblical exegesis and systematic theology. It is sometimes argued that a doctrine of infallibility imposed by systematic theology (or by the Reformed confessions) forces Biblical exegetes into a straightjacket; they are not allowed to come to conclusions that would conflict with the acceptance of the Bible as infallible.[9] It is senseless to deny this charge — and reverent exegetes should glory in it. If the Bible is true, then all it teaches must be true. Man's *first* calling in his approach to the Bible is not a "scientific" exegesis at all, but submission to the voice of God speaking as the Scriptures. In other words, the very fact that we have the Scriptures before us is proof that they are infallible, and any other conclusion arising from a so-called "objective" exegesis is flatly deceived — and deceiving.

If we recognize that every Word of God is an infallible Word, then we know that the Bible itself is the standard of infallibility against which all other notions of accuracy should be judged.[10] Operating with this God-honoring assumption, we can be certain that any exegetical conclusion that captures the meaning of a text constitutes nothing less than God's infallible Word. Whether it conforms to one's depraved, Enlightenment notions of "scientific accuracy" is meaningless and an affront to God.[11]

It was in the eighteenth and nineteenth centuries that men first began to look in earnest at the Bible as they would any other book, and treat it as they would any other book.[12] They felt that historic Christian orthodoxy was an affront to the Bible's meaning, and they threw overboard the idea of a supernatural, verbally inspired Bible as an impediment to getting at the actual, historical meaning of the text. *They were more convinced that they could recreate the history of two to three millennia ago than they were that the text before them is nothing less than the living Word of the Living God*. It was on these unbelieving assumptions that Protestant liberalism was able to undermine the Faith in the Western world. If the Bible is, as we believe, the very inspired Word of God, it cannot be treated like any other book.[13] The Scriptures come to us in human language, but this language was in fact created by God to suit His revelatory purposes. The Scriptures come to us by means of the writing of mere humans, but the mere humans were created by God to serve as vehicles for His revelation.[14] The Scriptures are transmitted to us in human history, but God predestines this history (and mainly His church in history) as the matrix within which His Word is preserved.[15] The Scriptures address all sorts of topics, heavenly, earthly, historical, ethical, scientific, artistic, and on and on; and the God Who inspired this Word shaped every single aspect of the universe of which His Word speaks. Therefore, we can never speak of any aspect of the Word of God as though it were contingent on the world, any more than we can speak of any aspect of the universe as though it were anything *other* than contingent on God. We do not judge the historical, ethical, scientific, and artistic aspects of Biblical revelation by some extra-scriptural standards or phenomena; we judge all extra-scriptural standards or phenomena by the Scriptures. For this reason we are obliged to join John William Burgon in affirming:

> ... THE BIBLE is none other than *the voice of Him that sitteth upon the throne!* Every Book of it, — every Chapter of it, — every Verse of it, — every word of it, — every syllable of it, — *where* are we to *stop*? — every letter of it — is the direct utterance of the Most High! .... The Bible is none other than *the Word of God:* not some part of it, more, some part of it, less; but all alike, the utterance of Him who sitteth upon the throne; — absolute, — faultless, — unerring, — supreme![16]

This is what we mean when we say the Bible is the infallible Word of God.

---

1 Andrew Sandlin, "The Word of the Sovereign is the True Battle for the Bible," in ed., Sandlin, *Keeping Our Sacred Trust* (Vallecito, CA, 1999), 10-25.

2 Richard A. Muller, *Post-Reformation Reformed Dogmatics* (Grand Rapids, 1993), 323.

3 John H. Gerstner, *A Bible Inerrancy Primer* (Winona Lake, IN, 1980).

4 Cornelius Van Til, *The Defense of the Faith* (Phillipsburg, NJ, 1967 edition), 236-241.

5 Charles C. Ryrie, "Update on Dispensationalism," in eds., Wesley R. Willis and John R. Master, *Issues in Dispensationalism* (Chicago, 1994), 15-27.

6 Meredith G. Kline, "Space and Time in the Genesis Cosmogony," from *Perspectives on Science and Christian Faith*, 48:2-15, 1996 [American Scientific Affiliation], published at http://mcgraytx.calvin.edu/ASA/PSCF3-96Klineold.html. Kline's earlier and less audacious piece is "Because It Had Not Rained," *Westminster Theological Journal* 20 (1958), 146-157.

7 Muller, *op. cit.*, 318-326, 378.

8 Cornelius Van Til, *op. cit.*, 44-45, 160.

9 Donald A. Hagner, "What is Distinctive About 'Evangelical' Scholarship?", *TSF Bulletin*, January-February, 1984, 6.

10 Noel Weeks, *The Sufficiency of Scripture* (Edinburgh, 1988), 3-36.

11 Rousas John Rushdoony, *Systematic Theology* (Vallecito, CA, 1994), 1:29.

12 W. Neil, "The Criticism and Theological Use of the Bible," in ed., S. L. Greenslade, *The Cambridge History of the Bible* (Cambridge, 1963), 3:238.

13 Edward F. Hills, *Believing Bible Study* (Des Moines, IA, 1967).

14 Benjamin Breckinridge Warfield, *The Inspiration and Authority of the Bible* (Phillipsburg, NJ, 1948), 156.

15 Theodore P. Letis, *The Ecclesiastical Text* (Philadelphia, 1997).

16 John W. Burgon, *Inspiration and Interpretation* (London, 1905), 86, emphasis in original.

Chapter 3

The Theology of Biblical Interpretation

The Inescapability of Interpretive Presuppositions

Every interpreter brings to his task certain presuppositions that shape the outcome of that task. The idea of an exegesis and interpretation void of presuppositions is a naive farce. Earlier liberal interpreters working on largely Enlightenment assumptions concluded that by dismissing the supernatural presuppositions of the church's exegetical and interpretative task throughout her history, they would arrive at the actual, historical meaning of the text.[1] To these interpreters, the church's orthodox presuppositions about the text clouded the text's actual meaning. Interestingly enough, the liberals' discarding the traditional and orthodox exegesis and interpretation did not lead to any sort of consensus about the so-called actual historic meaning of the text.[2] Rather, it simply demonstrated that these liberal interpreters had substituted an unbelieving, liberal interpretative presupposition for a believing, orthodox interpretative presupposition.

There is no neutrality in Biblical interpretation any more than there is in any other area of life. We should not derive from this fact what the so-called postmodernists do: that the Bible (like any other book) has no objective meaning, that its "meaning" is anchored in the mind of individual interpreters, which is to say, that it has no fixed meaning at all.[3] Rather, the variations in human interpretations derive from man's finitude and sin, not from a relative and changeable Biblical meaning. No doubt you have heard some "Spirit-led" Christians remark, "The Bible means one thing to one person and something else to another. It has different messages for different people." This is relativistic nonsense, sparked by man's lust for autonomy. It must be resisted at all costs.[4]

Reformation Presuppositions and Naiveté

Reformation exegetes and interpreters, because they had creditably abandoned the notion of Rome that tradition is an independent source of interpretation,[5] rarely recognized the role of presuppositions, even theological presuppositions, in the interpretative task.[6] They were still operating within a Christian social climate and orthodox theological climate which the medieval society had bequeathed to them[7] and thus it did not occur to them that differences of interpretation derive ultimately from differences in theological presuppositions, and not merely from a simple misunderstanding of the Bible. For this reason, as Steve Schlissel once observed, and as we noted earlier, we today must not begin by exegeting the Bible but by exegeting our presuppositions. Theological presuppositions shape exegetical conclusions — inescapably.

Every Christian who sits down to read his Bible, every minister who takes a text in hand, every Biblical scholar who pulls down his reference materials to begin a lexical study, brings to his task certain assumptions about the Bible, God, Jesus Christ, and the Christian message in general. These assumptions condition the way he reads and interprets the Bible and shape his understanding of it.

It is sometimes assumed that systematic theology is built on the results of Biblical theology which in turn are built on the results of exegesis.[8] One may erroneously be led to conclude from this sequence that exegesis does not presuppose a systematic theology. This is a naiveté that may lead to dangerous consequences. The exegete may think that his conclusions are not conditioned and shaped by theological presuppositions that constitute, at least in his mind, a systematic theology. He may then assume that he is doing nothing more than arriving at an "objective" understanding of the Bible to which theology itself makes no contribution. This will blind him to the very underlying assumptions in terms of which his exegesis operates. The Lutherans are often consistent in detecting this error, for while they believe that their confessions merely reproduce the teaching of the Bible, they understand that they read the Bible in terms of their confessions.[9] The fact recognized by these Lutherans is no less true of other Christian bodies. Everybody reads the Bible in terms of some confessional grid. *Theology always precedes Bible study.*

Creedalism, Confessionalism, and Presuppositions

It is often charged that orthodox interpreters exegete the Bible only to reaffirm what their confessional tradition already presumes, that Calvinists, for example, want only to buttress the Westminster Confession, Lutherans the Formula of Concord, Anglicans the Thirty-Nine Articles, and so forth. There is an element of truth in this charge, and we interpreters must constantly go back to the Bible to check all of our beliefs in terms of it. But the charge itself can be misleading, since it may hint that some sort of confessional or theological structure can be avoided. This is simply untrue. In fact, Christianity's creeds and confessions, while not infallible, are nonetheless signposts on the road of exegesis and interpretation.[10] If the standard conservative commentaries and Reformation confessions are like a yield sign, the ecumenical creeds of the first few Christian centuries are like a stop sign. We should be cautious in overturning a consensus of Bible-believing commentators (and this is really what the Reformation confessions are), and we must be positively unwilling to criticize ecumenical orthodoxy, hammered out in the early Christian creeds of the undivided church. We must constantly remember that ecumenical orthodoxy constitutes the core of Christianity: it defines the fundamentals of our religion. If the church has been mistaken in its fundamentals for the last 1800 years or so, we are left with the dire conclusion that the Christianity that has been practiced over the last two millennia has been mistaken at its very core. This is to deny that God has so overshadowed His church as to keep it from severe defection. God never promised to preserve His church from all error, or even from error in many matters; but He did promise that His Spirit would lead the apostles into all truth (*Jn. 16:13*); and if the church since the apostles has been misled on truth as fundamental to the Faith as the Trinity or the two natures of Christ, for example, we can say without fear of contradiction that there has been no Biblical Christianity for almost two millennia. For this reason, *Christian orthodoxy is a bedrock presupposition of Christian interpretation.* All of those in whom the Holy Spirit has done His deep work of regeneration inescapably operate on the presupposition of Christianity's truth.

Reformation Orthodoxy

But what is true of Christian orthodoxy is also largely true of Reformation orthodoxy.[11] We interpret the Bible in terms of the orthodoxy we believe it teaches. That this notion would sound odd or self-frustrating demonstrates the fuzzy thinking going on in the church today. When a newly converted individual is baptized and joins one of our churches, we do not hand him a Bible and say, "Read this Bible for yourself and interpret it just as you like; anybody who believes the Bible is welcome here, no matter what he believes." No, we instruct him in the Bible in terms of a particular orthodoxy springing from a particular interpretation. Reformation churches recognize, explicitly or not, that the Bible is the exclusive source of its interpretation (see chapter 1), and their work is to instill in members the interpretation they believe the Bible furnishes for itself. To assert differently is to assert pious nonsense. Consistently Protestant churches do not claim that their confessions, interpretations, and understanding of the Bible are infallible; but they do claim that the products of these practices are closer to what the Bible actually teaches than those in other sectors of the church. Obviously, if we did not believe this, we would not be Protestants. We believe that, on the whole, confessional Protestantism reproduces Biblical truth. This too is a presupposition in terms of which we read the Bible.

Revising Presuppositions

But to assert that we inescapably interpret the Bible in terms of presuppositions is not to say that those presuppositions can never change. This is why the notion of inescapable interpretative presuppositions is not a vicious cycle.[12] Just as God can resurrect a corpse, and breathe life into a dead soul, so He can change our own presuppositions. This, in fact, is precisely what He does (among other things) in regeneration. He reorients man's presuppositions about the Bible. Theretofore, man rebelled at God's Word; after regeneration, he submits to it. As the regenerate man approaches the Word of God time and again, this living (*Heb. 4:12*), divinely inspired and infallible document reshapes his thinking and life, including his presuppositions. Man is not caught in an historical warp from which he cannot escape. Man is a creature both of history and eternity. The ancient Greeks were wrong in denying the validity of history; they lusted for escape from the body in history because, for them, history and the body and the material world included man's distasteful, inferior features.[13] At the opposite end of the spectrum are the materialists, and especially the historicists. They, like Martin Heidegger, argue that the essence of man is historical being, that man is historical man and nothing else: existence precedes essence.[14] Both the ancient Greek view and the modern historicist view are anti-Christian to the core. History and historical existence are not inferior existences from which man should escape, as in the ancient Greek view, but aspects of God's good creation under His providential care. On the other hand, history is not all there is, and man is not only an historical being, as in the historicist view. Man is made in the image of God, and he must exist somewhere forever. He is a unified being of both history and eternity. Unlike God, he is a creature and is not eternal; but God determined at his creation that man, once created, would exist forever. Therefore, both history and eternity are important to man — because they are important to God, their Creator.

Divinely Conditioned

What does this mean with respect to interpreting the Bible? It means that while man is conditioned by history, he is conditioned ultimately by God. His approach to and interpretation of the Bible is an aspect of his conditioning. For the regenerate, sanctification includes a more accurate understanding of Biblical teaching. It is an aspect of what the Bible terms "growing in grace" (*2 Pet. 3:18*). Paul reprimands the Corinthians because their chronological age had outstripped their theological age (*1 Cor. 3:1-3*; see also *Heb. 5:11-14*). In other words, he was unable to teach them as much of the Faith as he wished, because they had not grown in grace and obedience. Sanctification includes increased Biblical understanding. This is true not only for the regenerate individual, but also for the church as a whole. It must progress in its understanding of the Bible and the Faith — and it has.

The Restorationist Error

This fact points to the serious error of those who, for example, lust for a restoration of the patristic era — roughly the first 500 years of the church.[15] They talk glowingly of the church fathers and, within certain constraints, they are justified in doing so. But from another and equally valid perspective, these early Christian writers were the church *babies*.[16] They lived within the first few centuries after the entire canon had been completed, and did not have time to develop a full-orbed systematic theology.[17] This is why Anselm's theology is far superior to Origen's and why Calvin's is far superior to Anselm's. But what is true of the relation between the Reformation and the patristic era is equally true of the relation between the modern and the Reformation era. Cornelius Van Til's apologetics is a significant improvement on Calvin's, just as R. J. Rushdoony's view of the law dwarfs Luther's. Maturity, including maturity in interpretation, occurs over time. And this is why interpretative progress is an aspect of Christian progress in general. We can expect that, over time, the church as a whole will arrive at a more accurate understanding of the Bible. We should expect that from three to five hundred years from now, those who follow us and are faithful to the Lord and His Word will outstrip our knowledge and accomplishments.[18]

Every generation must turn to the Word of God afresh for an even greater understanding of its truths. Nor does this imply any lack of respect for its predecessors; if its attitude is one of iconoclasm toward its reverent predecessors, it will cut out from beneath itself the very ground on which its expects to progress. We stand taller than our predecessors, not because we ourselves are taller, but because we can stand on their shoulders. A pigmy who stands on my shoulders will see more and farther than I, even though he is much shorter than I. We sail the boat of Christian interpretation squarely within the stream of Christian orthodoxy, but the boat does not stand still; it continues to move forward.[19]

The Inevitability of Scholasticism

The Reformation era was one of exciting, fresh exegetical insights after a long era of scholastic, medieval staleness. Yet, perhaps surprisingly, the seventeenth-century successors of the very Reformers who had decried the cold scholasticism of the medieval era developed scholastic forms of Reformation orthodoxy that in some ways exceeded anything that the medieval era had done. This should not shock us, and, within reason, there is nothing wrong with it. The Protestant dogmaticians who consolidated the gains of Reformation exegesis were only doing in the seventeenth century what the medieval scholastics had done with patristic orthodoxy. This is how interpretative and theological progress occurs. We stand on the shoulders of those who have gone before us. Every advance in Biblical interpretation creates a scholasticism of some sort, which remains largely undisturbed until it is subjected to a fresh, vigorous re-examination in light of the Bible. The products of Biblical interpretation must be placed into a systematic arrangement, and this demands scholasticism. Our objective, therefore, should never be to overthrow scholasticism as such, for this is impossible, but to press for a more Biblically faithful scholasticism.

To summarize: in the interpretative task, two factors should constantly be kept at the forefront of our minds. First, that we must operate in terms of theological presuppositions, primarily those of Christian orthodoxy. We can never escape presuppositions of some sort, and it is far preferable to operate explicitly in terms of the presuppositions of Christian orthodoxy than to try to recreate a "neo-orthodoxy" in every generation, a tack that tends to undermine the Faith. Second, we must constantly appeal to the Bible,

God's holy, living Word, which reorients us and refines our presuppositions and furnishes an increasingly greater understanding of God's written revelation within the bounds of Christian orthodoxy.

---

1 Alan Richardson, "The Rise of Modern Biblical Scholarship and Recent Discussion of the Authority of the Bible," in ed., S. L. Greenslade, *The Cambridge History of the Bible* (Cambridge, 1963), 3:299-305.

2 Gerhard Maier, *The End of the Historical-Critical Method* (St. Louis, 1974), 47-49.

3 Alan Jacobs, "Deconstruction," in eds., Clarence Walhout and Leland Ryken, *Contemporary Literary Theory: A Christian Appraisal* (Grand Rapids, 1991), 172-198.

4 On how doctrine is — and should be — formulated, see Alister McGrath, *The Genesis of Doctrine* (Grand Rapids, 1990), 35-80 and *passim*.

5 Yves Congar, *The Meaning of Tradition* (New York, 1964).

6 Peter Toon, *The Development of Doctrine in the Church* (Grand Rapids, 1979), 78.

7 On the continuity of the Reformation with the church catholic, see Jaroslav Pelikan, *Obedient Rebels* (New York and Evanston, 1964).

8 This is a typically fundamentalist notion. See Robert D. Bell, "Introduction: What Is Biblical Theology?", *Biblical Viewpoint*, Vol. XV, No. 2 [November 1981], 80-83. For a more thoughtful approach, see Klaus Bockmuehl, "The Task of Systematic Theology," in eds., Kenneth S. Kantzer and Stanley N. Gundry, *Perspectives in Evangelical Theology* (Grand Rapids, 1979), 3-14.

9 Erling T. Teigen, "Confessional Lutheranism versus Philippistic Conservatism," *Logia*, Vol. ii, No. 4 [October, 1993], 35.

10 Charles Augustus Briggs, *Theological Symbolics* (New York, 1914).

11 Jaroslav Pelikan, *Reformation of Church and Dogma (1300-1700)* (Chicago and London, 1984), 336-350.

12 J. I. Packer, "Infallible Scripture and the Role of Hermeneutics," in eds., D. A. Carson and John D. Woodbridge, *Scripture and Truth* (Grand Rapids, 1983), 348-353.

13 Andrew Louth, *The Origins of the Christian Mystical Tradition* (Oxford, 1981), 1.

14 Martin Heidegger, *Being and Time* (Albany, 1996).

15 On the restorationist lure, see Donald G. Bloesch, *The Future of Evangelical Christianity* (Garden City, NY, 1983), 85-91.

16 James B. Jordan, *The Liturgy Trap* (Niceville, FL, 1994), 66.

17 Jaroslav Pelikan, *Development of Christian Doctrine* (New Haven and London, 1969).

18 This is progress *within* the boundaries of the orthodox Faith, not outside it. The fact that genuine Christian progress occurs within orthodox boundaries is the conservative element countering the essential progressive element. See James Orr, *Progress of Dogma* (Old Tappan, NJ, n.d.), 17, 31.

19 Philip Schaff, *The Principle of Protestantism* (Philadelphia and Boston, 1964), 201.

Chapter 4

The Covenant and Biblical Interpretation

If, as we observed in the previous chapter, every act of interpretation presupposes a theology, we would be wise to inquire into the validity of that theology. Theology and interpretation are implied in one another. A sincere Biblical interpreter learns his theology from the Bible, and he approaches the Bible in terms of a particular theology. Interpretation and theology are, therefore, two fabrics woven into a single garment.

Reformed Christians interpret the Bible in terms of the covenant.[1] This is one reason we are called covenant theologians. Understand: we are not called covenant theologians merely because we derive a theology of the covenant from the Bible, but also because we approach the Bible in terms of the covenant. The Westminster Confession correctly observes that God has chosen to deal with man in terms of covenant.[2] If this is true, then we cannot understand the Bible as we should unless we approach it covenantally.

The Covenant Defined

What is a covenant? It is a solemn, *legally* binding agreement between either equals or unequals, binding them to a particular relation. Covenants are often bound by oath, even bloody oath. They solemnly hold the parties to certain requirements, and in terms and conditions that carry on to succeeding generations.[3] Covenants between God and man are always, of course, among unequals. God is the Creator, and man is the creature. For this reason, every divine-human covenant is initiated by God and is a gracious covenant. Even the legal dimension of the covenant is anchored in God's grace. For God is under no compulsion to make a covenant with man or anybody else. He has willingly condescended to covenant Himself with man — or with certain men.

The principal covenants in Scripture are the elective and redemptive covenants — the Adamic covenant (*Gen. 3:14-19*), the Noahic covenant (*Gen. 6:17-22; 9:1-17*), the Abrahamic covenant (*Gen. 17:1-14*), the Mosaic covenant (*Gen. 19*), the Davidic covenant (*2 Sam. 7:4-17*), and the new covenant (*Jer. 31:31-34*). The great elective and redemptive covenants of the Bible are actually separate historical manifestations of a single covenant of God with His chosen people. Some refer to this as the covenant of grace. This expression is perhaps superfluous, since all covenants of God with man are gracious covenants.

Covenant Theology and Biblical Interpretation

The significance of covenant theology for Biblical interpretation is that it constitutes the theology in terms of which we must interpret all the Bible. We do not mean by this that the covenant is what Rushdoony terms a "master principle," a particular motif by which we can understand everything in the Bible.[4] Rather, it is one overarching Biblical teaching that gives meaning to the Biblical data.

For one thing, the Bible itself is a covenant document. We speak of the Old and New Testaments, or covenants. Though these designations are frequently misused, it is quite true that the Bible furnishes us a record of God's covenant dealings with man — with His specially chosen people, and with the rest of the world. It is a record of God's covenant dealings. Even those who are not members of the covenant of grace, united to Christ by faith, are members of the covenant with the first (sinful) Adam. No man is outside the sphere of a covenant relationship with God. All who are Christ's stand in relation to Him, the Second Adam, as elect, redeemed, and obedient. All who are outside Christ stand in relation to Him as non-elect, unregenerate, and disobedient (*Rom. 5:12-21*).

The Unity of God's Plan

A fundamental Reformed truth of Biblical interpretation is the unity of God's plan of redemption and His dealings with man. God does not maintain and operate two separate elective and redemptive plans for two separate people with two separate laws and two separate destinies. This puts our interpretive approach squarely at odds with Dispensationalists, most Evangelicals, many Lutherans, and others. The issue is not fundamentally that they interpret the Bible differently; the issue is that their theology shapes their approach to the Bible in such as way as to render their interpretation of it incorrect. This interpretive error is most graphically demonstrated in the assumption that the Hebrew Old Testament represents a relatively inferior religion, law, and people. A consistently Reformed theological approach resists this notion at every point. The theological error leading to the interpretive error is reinforced by the description of the Hebrew books as the "Old Testament." Of course, the Bible itself nowhere refers to these books as the Old Testament any more than it refers to the Greek books as the "New Testament." Apparently it was Melito, Bishop of Sardis, who first designated these books the Old Testament to contrast them with the Greek apostolic writings that later came to be called the New Testament.[5] It was on the basis of the citation of Jeremiah 33:31-34 in Hebrews 8 and 10 that Origen denominated the last twenty-seven books of the Bible as the New Testament.[6] In this usage, "testament" is synonymous with "covenant," and this is in line with the Bible's usage. In other words, quite early, the church picked up the designation of the Hebrew aspect of the Bible as the old covenant and the Greek books as the new covenant.

The Old Testament Is Not the Old Covenant

This designation, arising from a particular theological presupposition, has led the church into numerous interpretive errors. The fact is that the Hebrew Scriptures pertain just as much to the new covenant as they do to the old covenant, and the Greek Scriptures pertain just as much to the old covenant as they do to the new covenant. As Rayburn has observed, the old and new covenants are not historical, and certainly not interpretive, distinctions, but subjective distinctions.[7] The old covenant is the sphere of unbelief, works-righteousness, and disobedience in any era, just as the new covenant is the sphere of faith, gracious justification, and obedience in any era. The old and new covenants are analogous to the old and new man, as used in Paul's writings (*Rom. 6:6; Col. 3:9-10; Eph. 4:22-24*). Noah, Enoch, Abraham, Isaac, David, and so forth were new covenant believers living in the Old Testament era (*Heb. 11*). The recipients of the Epistle to the Hebrews were in danger of becoming (or already had become) old covenant individuals living in the New Testament era.[8] The old and new covenants are not historical or canonical distinctions, but subjective distinctions. They describe individuals and groups of individuals in their covenant standing before God.

The same is true in Galatians. There the problem is largely with those who want to use law-keeping as the instrument of their justification (*5:4*). Certain false teachers were misusing the law. Paul uses the Old Testament account of Abraham's sons, Isaac and Ishmael, as an "allegory" for "the two covenants" (*4:24*). The first is related to Mt. Sinai, which leads to bondage; the second covenant, Isaac's covenant, relates to the "Jerusalem" which is above, is free, and which is the mother of us [Christians] all" (*v. 26*). These no doubt refer to what are elsewhere called the old covenant and the new covenant; but they certainly are not referring to the New Testament and the Old Testament. After all, both of these covenants are present in the Old Testament with two brothers! In other words, both the new covenant and the old covenant begin in the Old Testament. Paul tells us that Isaac was born again (*v. 29*). He tells us that the law itself teaches that there are two covenants (*v. 21*). One covenant leads to bondage (note also *3:23-24; 4:3, 9*). The other covenant, the new covenant, leads to promise and freedom (*v. 4:22-23, 26, 28, 30-31*). The new covenant is simply godly Old Testament religion!

New Covenant Religion of the Old Testament

The error in canonical designation reinforces the mistaken idea that the religion, law, and people to which the Hebrew

Scriptures pertain are somehow inferior to those to which the Greek Scriptures pertain. The fact is, however, that the true, faithful religion practiced in the Old Testament is not in substance different from the true, faithful religion practiced since Christ's incarnational and redemptive ministry. This is one of the principal themes of the book of Hebrews.

Similarly, the law given to the people of God in the Hebrew Scriptures is not somehow inferior to the law outlined in the Greek Scriptures. Jesus Christ Himself in the Sermon on the Mount (*Mt. 5:17-19*) argues with the greatest force for the authority of Old Testament law.[9] Likewise, the principal people of God in the Old Testament Scriptures, the devout Jews and Gentiles who placed faith in the Christ Who was to come, are not one iota qualitatively inferior to those Jews and Gentiles who place faith in Christ after His great, historic-redemptive work. It is true that God dealt chiefly with the Jews as His covenant people in the historical period covered by the Hebrew Scriptures, while, as a result of Christ's death, the covenant is now open to Gentiles as Gentiles: Gentiles no longer must become Jews to enter the covenant (*Eph. 2:11-22*). It is a frequent, but serious, error, however, to suppose that the Greek Scriptures portray a new form of religion in which the Jews have been forever set aside (this is plainly contrary to St. Paul's teaching in Romans 11[10]), or that the Hebrews' covenant is primarily about racial Jewishness. All to the contrary, as Paul teaches in Galatians 3:6-8 and elsewhere, that the Gentiles were to be a part of the covenant people of God was of the very essence of the gospel.[11]

Old covenant religion and new covenant religion run throughout the Bible, side by side — and throughout human history. Today the entire human race is split into old and new covenant members (*Gal. 3:22-4:31*). Those who tie the old covenant order almost exclusively to Old Testament Israel are simply mistaken. Both the new covenant and the old covenant began in the Garden of Eden. Abel was the first leading new covenant figure in history (*Heb. 11:4*). Old covenant religion certainly existed among Old Testament Israel, but so did new covenant religion.

Some, moreover, hold the mistaken view that the old covenant order was put away in the destruction of Jerusalem in A. D. 70. The old covenant order will not be put away definitively and finally until the final judgment. But a little of the old covenant order is put away every time an individual is saved — he is translated from the old covenant order to the new covenant order.

New Covenant Interpretation

How does this theological perspective relate to Biblical interpretation? It means, among other things, that the Hebrew Scriptures are Christian Scripture no less than the Greek Scriptures. In other words, as Joe Braswell once observed, the entire Bible is a new covenant book. The Hebrew Scriptures do not articulate a different or inferior message to which the Greek Scriptures stand in contrast. In simpler terms, all of the Bible is the Word of God, setting forth a unified, single message.

This naturally leads to the second implication: the Hebrew Scriptures are no less authoritative than the Greek Scriptures. Unless the Scriptures themselves teach us that certain aspects of revelation are no longer applicable, we may presume that all of the Scriptures — Hebrew and Greek — are authoritative in the lives of Christians and the modern world in general.[12]

Very early in the patristic church, many theologians blunted the force of Hebrew revelation by allegorizing it. They were convinced that only in this way could they preserve those Hebrew Scriptures as revelation attesting to Christ.[13] They were quite correct in recognizing that the entire Bible is Christological, that all of it is a testimony to Christ. They were quite wrong, however, in thinking that this Christological interpretation had to be attained at the expense of the obvious meaning of the text. The Reformation helped to correct this error.[14]

Likewise, those today in the so-called "redemptive-historical" school often dismiss the eternal authority of the Mosaic judicial law (see Appendix 2); they hold that to retain it is to apply it "non-Christologically."[15] In other words, they have decided beforehand exactly what a "Christological" interpretation must be and then they do away with certain divine commandments (the civil law, for instance) on that basis. We all acknowledge, of course, that the Old Testament everywhere testifies of Jesus Christ in one way or another, and that the church of the Greek Scriptures has indeed become the fulfillment of the church of the Hebrew Scriptures. But even in the Hebrew Scriptures, the jurisdiction of the judicial law of God was not limited to Israel; all people everywhere stood under its authority, and this is precisely what the New Testament teaches (*Rom. 3:19*).

These are only two examples of how mistaken theological presuppositions lead to a mistaken interpretation. This naturally leads to a mistaken application. It is vital to note that in these cases the Bible itself does not rescind certain Biblical commands; rather, men have allowed their theological presuppositions to cloud their minds about the full authority of Scripture. Their theology clouds their interpretation, which in turn distorts their actions.

Replacement Theology

The Biblical understanding of the covenant does away with all main forms of "replacement theology." The New Testament has not replaced the Old Testament. The gospel has not replaced the law. The Christian church has not replaced Christian Israel. The heavenly has not replaced the earthly. And the new covenant has not replaced the old covenant.

The entire Bible, both the Hebrew and Greek Scriptures, is God's covenant revelation. A fundamental rule of interpretation is that all of the Bible is the Word of God and it speaks one revelation, one message, one law; it addresses one redeemed people and one unredeemed people; and it establishes one religion. This is a bedrock theological presupposition undergirding the interpretive endeavor.

---

[1] Berkhof, *Systematic Theology* (Grand Rapids, 1938 edition), 262-264.
[2] Westminster Confession of Faith, Ch. 7, Sec. 1.
[3] O. Palmer Robertson, *The Christ of the Covenants* (Phillipsburg, NJ, 1980), 3-15.
[4] Rousas John Rushdoony, *Systematic Theology* (Vallecito, CA, 1994), 1:107-111.
[5] Daniel P. Fuller, *The Unity of the Bible* (Grand Rapids, 1992), 29, 65-66.
[6] Walter Kaiser, *Toward an Old Testament Theology* (Grand Rapids, 1978), 231-232.
[7] Robert S. Rayburn, "The Contrast Between the Old and New Covenants in the New Testament," doctoral dissertation, University of Aberdeen, 1978.
[8] *idem.*, "Hebrews," in ed., Walter A. Elwell, *Evangelical Commentary on the Bible* (Grand Rapids, 1989), 1124-1149.
[9] Greg L. Bahnsen, *Theonomy in Christian Ethics* (Phillipsburg, 1984 edition).
[10] John Murray, *The Epistle to the Romans* (Grand Rapids, 1965), 2:91-96.
[11] Jeffrey S. Siker, *Disinheriting the Jews* (Louisville, KY, 1991), 37.
[12] Rousas John Rushdoony, *Institutes of Biblical Law* (no loc., 1973).
[13] Jaroslav Pelikan, *The Emergence of the Catholic Tradition* (Chicago and London, 1971), 81.
[14] Gustaf Aulen, *Reformation and Catholicity* (Edinburgh and London, 1962), 127.
[15] Dan G. McCartney, "The New Testament Use of the Pentateuch: Implications for the Theonomic Movement," in eds., William S. Barker and W. Robert Godfrey, Theonomy: A Reformed Critique (Grand Rapids, 1990), 148.

Appendix 1
Two Paradigms for Adherents of *Sola Scriptura*

The Protestant Reformation unwaveringly emphasized *sola Scriptura* — Scripture alone. Certain portions of the late medieval church had posited (whether explicitly or implicitly) ecclesiastical tradition as an independent source of authority. The Reformers opposed this: for example, Mariology, veneration of the saints, purgatory, and indulgences had no part in the Bible's revelation. To hold, as Rome did, that they comprised ingredients of the Christian Faith was to undercut the gospel. The Latin slogan *sola Scriptura* meant that the Bible alone is the church's sole, ultimate authority. All other authorities — church, state, parents, and so on — do not speak a divine word. Each holds only a derivative authority, subordinate to the Sacred Scriptures.[1]

It is commonly held by both Protestants and Roman Catholics alike that *sola Scriptura* was an innovation the Reformers introduced into Western Christianity. Actually, this is not the case at all. There was wide acceptance of *sola Scriptura* in certain sectors of the late medieval church.[2] Unfortunately, there was also the viewpoint against which the Reformers were reacting — ecclesiastical tradition as a separate, independent authority.

At the Council of Trent, the Roman Catholic answer to the Protestant Reformation, the Latin church codified the "two-source" theory of revelational authority: both the Sacred Scriptures and unwritten tradition handed down in the church were deemed equally authoritative.[3] It is this theory which the original Protestants and their successors vigorously opposed. To embrace the "two-source" theory of divine revelation, they believed, was to erase the Creator-creature distinction.[4] This is the great error of Tridentine Roman Catholicism, and it is parallel to its twin, salvation by both faith *and* works. Both erase the Creator-creature distinction. This is a dangerous form of *synergism*. The Protestants recognized that man and God cooperate no more in salvation than they do in revelation. God's *revelation* to man is an absolute revelation in whose origin man does not cooperate. God's *salvation* of man is an absolute salvation in whose origin man does not cooperate. Man is the *object* of both revelation and salvation, not the *origin*. *Sola Scriptura* guards the Creator-creature distinction as it relates to God's objective revelation to man in the Bible.[5]

Reformers, Not Revolutionaries

In contesting Rome's "two-source" theory of revelation, the Protestant Reformers were by no means arguing that the Western church's doctrine was altogether erroneous. The Reformers were just that — reformers, not revolutionaries. They were quite willing to affirm the inherited ecumenical orthodoxy of the Latin Church, for instance. The Reformers were all Trinitarians, and affirmed the dogma of the ecumenical councils.[6] They did this not because they acknowledged the ultimate authority of church councils, but because they believed that these early ecumenical councils expressed Biblical teachings on the core elements of Christianity.

Radicals, Not Reformers

This distinguished the Protestant Reformation from the so-called Radical Reformation, the Anabaptists, the Unitarians, and so on.[7] These latter also affirmed a sort of *sola Scriptura*. To them, it meant that the Bible alone is our authority and, *therefore*, orthodox Christianity is suspect. Many of the radical reformers questioned or denied the Trinity. The Protestant Reformers rightly found this abhorrent — no less abhorrent, and perhaps more abhorrent, than the "two-source" theory of revelation by Rome. While Rome believed in a "two-source" theory of revelation, the radical reformers believed in no tradition of any kind. The Protestants, however, believed in a *Biblical* tradition. A tradition gaining great currency in the church that flows out of the Sacred Scriptures itself is authoritative because it is Biblical.[8] Therefore, the Reformers and their successors did not deny a positive role to tradition. In fact, Lutheran theologian Martin Chemnitz, in his massive refutation of the Council of Trent, conspicuously acknowledged this crucial role of tradition.[9] So did the Protestant Irish Articles of Religion, which explicitly affirmed the early ecumenical creeds.[10] John Calvin himself arranged his great systematic theology, *Institutes of the Christian Religion,* around the Apostles Creed. All of the early Protestants argued in favor of ancient catholic orthodoxy.

Regula Fidei

This understanding of the Bible's authority and the godly ecclesiastical tradition that flows out of it created a particular standard of interpretation, a *regula fidei,* or divine rule. This was a certain traditional *way* of interpreting the Bible. Luther, Calvin, and other Reformers gleaned great nuggets from the Word of God that had been obscured by the highly static exegesis of the late medieval period. For one thing, they recovered the Pauline-Augustinian doctrine of justification by faith alone. But they were not revolutionaries. They believed in a *traditional* exegesis bounded by ancient catholic orthodoxy.

This is exactly what the patristic church had held. It did not hold the later Roman Catholic idea of Scripture and tradition as separate sources of authority, but neither did it hold the Radical Reformation view that the Bible overthrows all tradition. It held that the Bible alone is our ultimate objective authority, but that there is a legitimate, *traditional* way of interpreting the Bible.[11]

Hermeneutics

Today we hear a great about "hermeneutics." This is really just a sophisticated term for interpretation — usually, the interpretation of the Bible. Even among those who hold to the highest view of the Bible's formal authority, there is great disagreement on its interpretation. I refer not mainly to the conclusions of that interpretation, for instance, Calvinism versus Arminianism, amillennialism versus postmillennialism, dispensationalism versus covenant theology, infant baptism versus professors' baptism. Rather, I refer more fundamentally to the rules that govern interpretation itself. Different views of these rules lead to different interpretations of specific passages of the Bible and to different theological views.

Some hold, for example, that the Bible must be interpreted in its original historical context (as best as we today can ascertain that) and has a single intended meaning. Others agree that it should be interpreted in its original historical context, but hold to a *sensus plenior*: it can have more than one intended meaning. Still others hold that all interpretation must be *canonically* contextual — that is, the entire Bible is the context within which a single text is interpreted. Still others are less committed to the specific historical meaning at the time the Bible was penned than to an ultimate, general meaning that God intended to transcend any particular historical situation. Some even wish to distinguish between meaning and significance! These are only a few of the hermeneutical "options" among those who affirm the infallibility of the Bible. Among those who do not affirm the infallibility of the Bible, the hermeneutical options are, unfortunately, even greater.

Historic Versus Innovative Exegesis

More basic and more crucial than any of these differences is that great distinction among Protestant interpreters between those who embrace the original Protestant view, that is, a traditional *way* of interpreting the Bible, and those who have sided, intentionally or not, with the Radical Reformation, which does not recognize the bounds of orthodoxy in the interpretative endeavor. For purposes of classification, we may label these views as *historic* exegesis and *innovative* exegesis. Of course, those who embrace historic exegesis do not deny the permissibility — or even the necessity — of exegetical innovation. They simply oppose innovation *that would overturn orthodox Christianity.*[12] Similarly, adherents of innovative exegesis do not wish to throw Christian orthodoxy overboard; they may hold to certain orthodox tenets, but the crucial point is that they are willing to subject those tenets to what they consider contrary exegetical evidence.

Protestant Liberalism

Some examples will suffice. Protestant liberals of the late eighteenth and early nineteenth centuries embraced an assertedly "neutral," "objective," "scientific" form of grammatical-historical exegesis. That meant finding out what the Scriptures meant when they were originally written. Almost all liberal exegetes were committed to this approach.[13] These liberal Protestants were quite willing, if necessary, to throw overboard essential tenets of orthodox Christianity — the Trinity, the deity of Christ, the inspiration and infallibility of the Bible, and so on — if the conclusions of their grammatical-historical exegesis warranted this abandonment. Superficially, they seemed to be carrying on the best tradition of the Protestant Reformers, who lent great weight to the original meaning of Biblical passages and their historic context. What the liberal Protestants did not share with the Protestant Reformers, however, was a commitment to orthodox Christianity. Therefore, they were quite willing to eviscerate orthodox Christianity on the cutting table of grammatical-historical exegesis. The modern liberal Protestant, James Barr, has suggested that this is merely the consistent outcome of the grammatical-historical exegesis employed by the original Reformers.[14] Whatever may be the merit of that suggestion, it is certain that the Reformers themselves would have found it abhorrent. They were categorically devoted to orthodox Christianity and would have found it astounding that Biblical exegesis may overturn orthodox Christianity. That, however, is precisely the viewpoint of the liberal innovative exegetes.

Sectarianism

A more conservative version emerged among those who are willing to throw the Christian creeds overboard if they are convinced those creeds can be shown at variance with the Bible's teaching. A most flagrant example of this was Alexander Campbell, founder of the so-called "Church of Christ":

> I have endeavored to read the scriptures as though no one had read them before me ... and as much on my guard against reading them to-day, through the medium of my own views yesterday, or a week ago, as I am against being influenced by any foreign name, authority, or system whatever.[15]

This is an astounding statement, but quite consistent if one denies the need for a traditional method of interpreting the Bible.

Consistent Preterism

Another example of innovative exegesis is in the so-called "consistent Preterist" school of recent years. Most of its supporters are willing to jettison the physical second coming of Christ and the physical resurrection of the saints, holding that these events occurred in or about the destruction of Jerusalem in A. D. 70.[16] This clearly deviates from the Christian doctrine expressed in the early ecumenical creeds, and the "consistent Preterists" acknowledge this deviation. They argue, however, that this deviation is justified on the ground that the Bible, in fact, requires just such a deviation.

There is no longer a traditional method of interpreting the Bible among the *innovative* exegetes; each exegete, as long as he practices his craft properly, is free to arrive at any conclusions, as long as he can justify them Biblically.

Historic Exegesis

The *historic* exegetes find this approach most troubling — even dangerous. While they uncompromisingly embrace *sola Scriptura,* and oppose Rome's "two-source" theory of revelation, they equally oppose the idea that a few isolated individuals should be permitted to overthrow the time-tested understanding of Scripture. In Thomas Sowell's notable language, they embrace the "constrained vision" of humanity.[17] This is the idea that knowledge is dispersed widely, among many people in the contemporary world, as well as over many previous generations. They do not believe that the highest form of knowledge inheres in a few bright individuals of any age. For the *historic* exegetes, this is another way of saying that there is a traditional *way* of interpreting the Bible. This *way* is really the bounds of historic, orthodox Christianity. Princeton theologian and exegete Charles Hodge was one of the leading proponents of this view:

> Protestants admit that there has been an uninterrupted tradition of truth from the protoevangelium to the close of the Apocalypse, so that there has been a stream of traditionary teaching flowing through the

> Christian church from the day of Pentecost to the present time. This tradition is so far a rule of faith that nothing contrary to it can be true. Christians do not stand isolated, each holding his own creed. They constitute one body, having one common creed. Rejecting that creed, or any of its parts, is the rejection of the fellowship of Christians, incompatible with the communion of saints, or membership in the body of Christ. In other words, Protestants admit that there is a common faith of the Church, which no man is at liberty to reject and be a Christian.[18]

Hodge succinctly expresses the Protestant view that Biblical tradition affirmed by the church catholic is an inviolable rule of faith. We are not free to abandon it, even in our Biblical exegesis.

Exegesis within this Christian tradition is desirable, even if it sometimes errs. While, for example, many of the patristic exegetes may have relied a little too heavily on a mystical and, therefore, fanciful exegesis, those who remained within the fold of the orthodox faith were practicing a legitimate *Christian* exegesis, no matter how erroneous their specific conclusions may have been. Likewise, while exegetes during the time of the Protestant Reformation may have relied a little too heavily on the immediate historical context of specific Biblical passages (not taking into account, for example the entire range of the Bible), they stayed within the confines of orthodox Christianity, and thus their exegesis was legitimate *Christian* exegesis. This traditional *way* of interpreting the Bible holds that the ancient ecumenical orthodoxy is an *implicit* deduction from the Bible's *explicit* teaching. In the language of the Presbyterians' Westminster Confession of Faith, it is "good and necessary consequence." If, therefore, ancient catholic orthodoxy is what the Bible itself implicitly teaches, to interpret the Bible contrary to that orthodoxy is to wrongly interpret the Bible.

Historical exegesis and innovative exegesis are, in fact, two distinct, definable paradigms, even visions. They constitute different approaches to the Bible and to its interpretation and, in many cases, lead to different, sometimes radically different, conclusions.

---

[1] J. I. Packer, "'Sola Scriptura' in History and Today," in ed., John Warwick Montgomery, *God's Inerrant Word* (Minneapolis, 1974), 43-62.

[2] Alister McGrath, *The Intellectual Origins of the European Reformation* (Grand Rapids, 1987), 148-151.

[3] Philip Schaff, *The Creeds of Christendom* (Grand Rapids [1931], 1990), 2:80.

[4] Cornelius Van Til, *The Doctrine of Scripture* (no loc., 1967), 35.

[5] Auguste Lecerf, *An Introduction to Reformed Dogmatics* (Grand Rapids [1949], 1981), 294-301.

[6] Charles Augustus Briggs, *Theological Symbolics* (New York, 1914), 310.

[7] Harold O. J. Brown, *Heresies* (Garden City, NY, 1984), 326-327.

[8] Philip Schaff, *The Principle of Protestantism* (Philadelphia and Boston, 1964), 115-117.

[9] Martin Chemnitz, *Examination of the Council of Trent* (St. Louis, 1971), 1:235-236, 249-250, 258, 267-271.

[10] Schaff, *Creeds*, 3:528.

[11] J. N. D. Kelly, *Early Christian Doctrines* (New York, 1960 edition), 33.

[12] James Orr, *Progress of Dogma* (Old Tappan, NJ, n.d.), 17, 31.

[13] James Farrar, *History of Interpretation* (London, 1886), xxv-xxvi.

[14] James Barr, *Beyond Fundamentalism* (Philadelphia, 1984), 173.

[15] Cited in Nathan O. Hatch, "The Christian Movement and the Demand for a Theology of the People," in ed., D. G. Hart, *Reckoning With the Past* (Grand Rapids, 1995), 171.

[16] R. C. Leonard and J. E. Leonard, *The Promise of His Coming* (Chicago, 1996).

[17] Thomas Sowell, *A Conflict of Visions* (New York, 1987).

[18] Charles Hodge, *Systematic Theology* (Grand Rapids, 1981), 1:113-114.

Appendix 2

A Note on Redemptive-Historical Interpretation

One of the greatest Biblical theologians the Reformed Faith ever produced was Geerhardus Vos, professor of Biblical theology at Princeton. In the last few years of the nineteenth century until his retirement in 1932, Vos was the leading proponent of the redemptive-historical method of interpretation. In large part, Dutch Biblical theologian Herman Ridderbos later adopted this view, though apparently somewhat independently. Its leading proponent today is Westminster Seminary professor Richard Gaffin. The exegesis and theology of all three of these men are superior — and sometimes dazzling. The fresh way in which they approach the Scriptures often yields deep theological insights. Usually these insights spring from the practice of the redemptive-historical method itself. What is it?

The Method Defined

Reacting against the rather scholastic, a-historical approach of much of Reformed exegesis and theology, the practitioners of the redemptive-historical method perceive the Bible primarily in terms of its own history. The Bible, they note, is not a theological textbook but a divinely inspired account of certain discrete historical events, preeminently the great events surrounding Jesus Christ's great redemptive complex: His life, death, resurrection, ascension, and second coming. Gaffin explains:

> Specifically, the focus or orientation of Scripture in all its parts is the history of God's accomplishment of the redemption of his covenant people, which reaches its climax in the work of the incarnate Christ. So far as its content is concerned, biblical revelation is redemptive-historical (or covenantal) and christocentric.

> What needs to be made clear is that for Vos, *this generalization holds for biblical revelation in its entirety.* His point is not that by far the largest part of Scripture or its main emphasis concerns the redemptive work of Christ while the other, less prominent portions are basically independent of this concern, related to redemption only indirectly or not at all. Rather, in its way, *every single aspect or strand in the rich diversity of biblical revelation is oriented to salvation in Christ.* The death and resurrection of Christ constitutes the focal point of all biblical revelation.[1]

Revelation is distinctly *organic.* It unfolds historically, that is, within the historical period described by Scripture: it "comes in a historically progressive fashion."[2] As it moves forward in its description of history, it progressively reveals its message; that message comes to fulness in the New Testament epistles of Paul. Because of the historically shaped character of Biblical revelation, practitioners of the redemptive-historical method devote great attention to the historically shaped character of the text: its human authors, composition, style, and so forth. They are quick to dissociate this preoccupation from the theologically liberal diminution of Biblical authority on similar historical grounds. For its orthodox Reformed supporters, a high degree of inspiration is not jeopardized by an intense interest in the Bible's historical nature. In fact, they argue that *only* such an interest can bring to light the glory of the inspired Scripture.[3]

Insights of the Redemptive-Historical Method

This approach leads to some interesting, and often dramatic, insights. For instance, one conclusion of Gaffin's *Resurrection and Redemption: A Study in Paul's Soteriology*[4] is that the traditional Reformed *ordo salutis* (order of salvation) as it pertains to individuals has New Testament, or at least Pauline, soteriology quite wrong. The Biblical depiction of the individual's salvation is not one of a sequence of divine acts: regeneration, justification, sanctification, glorification, and so on. Rather, these are all facets of salvation simultaneously imparted at the sinner's union with Christ. Gaffin, following Vos, marshals extensive exegetical evidence that it is specifically union with the *resurrected Christ* — that is, in all of His resurrection *power* — that imparts salvation to the heretofore unbeliever. This implies, among other things, that Gaffin is willing to rethink the traditional Reformed idea that regeneration precedes and causes man's faith, usually considered the instrumental cause of justification.[5]

Another interesting feature of the redemptive-historical method is that it sees Paul and the modern New Testament interpreter as contemporary, as far as their approach to the interpretive task is concerned. Vos, Ridderbos, and Gaffin see Paul not merely as an instrument of divine inspiration, but as a *theologian* in his own right.[6] The gospels give us an account of the great redemptive complex, and Paul is their primary theological interpreter.[7] In short, Paul is a systematic theologian. While, of course, Paul wrote under divine inspiration and is, in this sense, qualitatively different from today's interpreters, he and they are interpreters together of Christ's great redemptive complex on which the entire Bible centers. Paul is not only our teacher; he is also our partner in the interpretive task.[8]

This entire paradigm is possible because the redemptive-historical method shifts attention from man's existential situation to the specific, concrete, historical work of Christ and His great redemptive complex. Vos, Ridderbos, and Gaffin argue that this great Christological redemptive complex — and it alone — is the matrix within which man's existential salvation occurs. The issue is not an individual *ordo salutis*. The issue is union with the resurrected Christ, and all that this implies.

The redemptive-historical method is a powerful reaction to the highly existential form of Christianity that arose in the late eighteenth and early nineteenth centuries and, indeed, survives to this day. Salvation is not mainly about my own personal dilemma and how to get out of it. Rather, salvation is about union with the resurrected Christ and the great work of redemption, which He accomplished in time and history.

Not only so, the redemptive-historical method presents a healthy alternative to an excessive scholasticism in both theology and in the church. Scholasticism, while inevitable, is tempted to reduce the Faith to arbitrarily assigned theological categories, diverting attention from the *kind* of book the Bible really is: a record of revelation-history. In Gaffin's words, "[T]he history of redemption [is] the subject matter or focus of the entire biblical record . . . . [A]ny theological reflection basing itself on biblical interpretation must recognize and work from out of this redemptive-historical framework. The redemptive-historical perspective is an indispensable horizon for understanding Scripture in part or as a whole."[9] This approach creditably diverts interpreters from abstract theological categories and re-focuses their attention on the revelation of the Bible itself.

Omitting the Post-Biblical History of Interpretation

Despite these strengths, the redemptive-historical method manifests certain troubling, and in some cases fatal, weaknesses. First, this method exalts history, but only a particular epoch of history, namely, the period covered by the Biblical records. It gives little attention to history since the closing of the canon, particularly with respect to the history of interpretation. One need not agree that "church history is the history of the exposition of Scripture"[10] to recognize the vital role that development of doctrine historically should play (and actually does play, whether we want it to or not) within the church in our present interpretation of Scripture. A development of orthodoxy, as well as Christian exegesis of the Bible, is not a factor that we can simply jettison. We confront Scripture in a particular historical context, and part of that context is a development of doctrine and exegesis within the church. The redemptive-historical method, while strongly historical with reference to the Biblical era, is decidedly a-historical with reference to the subsequent era of Biblical interpretation. In this point, at least, it seems heavily influenced by Enlightenment presuppositions, which attempted to wipe away understanding as it has developed historically and commit that understanding to a few extant, bright minds.[11]

Ironically, therefore, the redemptive-historical method is anything but historical as it pertains to interpretation within the full horizon of the "history of redemption," that is, the entire interadvental era.

Truncating the Biblical Message

Second, the redemptive-historical method forces the revelation of the Bible into an arbitrary, pre-assigned Procrustean bed. It sees the entire Bible in terms of redemption. But the Bible itself simply will not permit this reduction. The Bible is largely, though not exclusively, about redemption; and the teachings of the Bible pertaining to redemption depict it more broadly than the redemptive-historical method recognizes.[12] *Not redemption as such, but the Triune God Himself is the interpretive theme of the Bible*[13] — particularly the sovereignty of God in the affairs of creation, and preeminently man. Man's pre-fall task was to exercise dominion in the earth under his God's authority. When man fell into sin, God did not abandon His plan for man, but rather instituted redemption as the only means whereby man could be *restored* to this calling. The sovereign authority of the Triune God in the earth mediated by humans in submission to Him — and not redemption as such — is the Bible's guiding premise. Redemption is not the end, but the means to that end.

The redemptive-historical method seems to honor Christ by interpreting everything in the Bible through a redemptive grid, but in reality this truncates the full-orbed message of the Bible. For example, Vos, in his treatment of the Mosaic economy, devotes nearly forty pages to the ritual or ceremonial law, and *not a single page* to the civil law.[14] This surely is an imbalanced view of the revelation as we find it in the Old Testament, but it is plausible given the redemptive-historical method's presupposition of redemption as the theme in terms of which the entire Bible must be interpreted.

In this, too, the redemptive-historical method is ironic, in that, while it justifiably criticizes the abstractionism of much of Reformed systematic theology, it mires itself in one of the greatest abstractionisms of all — erecting a single master principle to which the entire Bible must give tribute. It neglects the only possible guiding theme of the Bible's message: the Triune God Himself.

Limiting Biblical Infallibility

Finally, an interpretive method oriented to such a narrow focus cannot escape a truncation of Biblical authority itself. In other words, any interpretive approach which narrows the focus of the Biblical message must, if consistently held, narrow the focus of its authority. This is just what happens with the most consistent expression of the redemptive-historical method, particularly as authority elates to truthfulness, or infallibility. "Is it possible to make a theory of inspiration," Ridderbos asks rhetorically, "in which not the nature of Scriptures themselves, but our theological postulates about what inspiration ought to be define the concept of authority and the inspiration of the Scriptures?"[15] He makes clear that the answer for which he is looking is, No: "[T]he authority [of the Bible] must be approached from the history of revelation and salvation itself."[16] Since redemptive history is the entire focus of the Bible, we must interpret its authority and truthfulness in terms of that focus. The *a priori* for assessing Biblical truthfulness is not the presupposition that the Bible as the Word of God can speak in no other way than infallibly; that would be to short-circuit its redemptive-historical message. Rather, the presupposition must be the Bible's redemptive-historical focus:

> We cannot say everything of Scripture that we say of the word of God, nor can we identify the apostles and prophets during their writing with the Holy Spirit. The word of God exists in eternity, is perfect. But Scripture is neither eternal nor perfect.... The fact is that the infallibility of Scripture has in

> many respects a character other than that which a theoretical concept of inspiration or infallibility, detached from its purpose and empirical reality, would like to demand.[17]

This consistent redemptive-historical approach to the truthfulness of Sacred Scripture not only undercuts the notion of that Scripture as a plenarily infallible word on the ground of its being the very Word of God. In addition, it consoles itself that it is only taking a cue from the very character of the Bible itself, which permits such a diminution of truthfulness. *If the message is exclusively redemptive-historical, the focus of its truthfulness must be exclusively redemptive-historical.* This warps the message of the Bible at its very source. In Shepherd's words, the authority of the message rests no longer on its source (God Himself), but on its content (an allegedly exclusive redemptive-historical focus).[18] Devotees of the redemptive-historical approach miss the fact that their own orientation constitutes an *a priori* judgment about the kind of book the Bible is — "redemptive-historical" — and, like all other interpretive schools, brings to its task certain assumptions that shape its exegetical and theological conclusions. The question is not whether we can avoid a view of inspiration "detached," in Ridderbos's language, "from its purpose and empirical reality." Every view of inspiration springs from a presupposition about the nature of the Triune God and a Christian life-system. There is no such thing as a purely inductive theory of Biblical inspiration or authority.[19] We cannot console ourselves by arguing that our view of truthfulness which limits it to a redemptive-historical focus is simply a conclusion from an investigation of the Bible's content. We begin, as Steve Schlissel asserts, not by exegeting the Bible, but by exegeting our presuppositions.[20] Those presuppositions, in the case of the redemptive-historical method, narrow the scope of the Bible's truthfulness by narrowing the scope of its message. If the Bible is all about redemption, then its truthfulness relates only to redemption. If, by contrast, it is all about God's regulating man as His creature (and redemption certainly is an aspect of that regulation), its truthfulness must extend equally to every part of it. This plenary infallibility cannot be a feature of any *consistent* expression of redemptive-historical interpretation.

Thus, despite its valuable contributions, the redemptive-historical method, in largely dismissing the history of interpretation; in forcing all Biblical data into a rather arbitrary theological grid; and, most significantly, in limiting the scope of Biblical truthfulness to its alleged redemptive-historical focus, creates as many interpretive problems as it solves. Further, it leaves the church with less than a full-orbed message by which to press the claims of Christ's kingdom in the earth.

---

1 Richard B. Gaffin, Jr., "Introduction," *Redemptive History and Biblical Interpretation: The Shorter Writings of Geerhardus Vos*, ed. Gaffin (Phillipsburg, NJ, 1980), xv-xvi, emphasis supplied.

2 *ibid.*, xvi.

3 *ibid.*, xxiii.

4 (Phillipsburg, NJ, 1978, 1987).

5 *ibid.*, 135-143.

6 Vos's classic on this topic is *The Pauline Eschatology* (Phillipsburg, NJ, [1930] 1987). Ridderbos's penetrating work is *Paul: An Outline of His Theology* (Grand Rapids, 1975).

7 Herman N. Ridderbos, *When the Time Had Fully Come* (Jordan Station, Ontario, [1957] 1982), 49.

8 Richard B. Gaffin, Jr., "Geerhardus Vos and the Interpretation of Paul," in ed., E. R. Geehan, *Jerusalem and Athens* (Phillipsburg, NJ, 1971), 232.

9 *idem.*, "Introduction," xx.

10 Gerhard Ebeling, *The Word of God and Tradition* (Philadelphia, 1964, 1968), 11.

11 Alister McGrath, *The Genesis of Doctrine* (Grand Rapids, 1990), 132-138.

12 Cornelius Van Til, *Christian Theistic Ethics* (Phillipsburg, NJ, 1980), 82-84.

13 "Any theology that seeks as its basic principle of interpretation Christ rather than the Triune God seeks to reduce God to His relationship to man rather than to establish God Himself as the basic principle of interpretation," Rousas John Rushdoony, *By What Standard?* (Vallecito, [1958] 1995), 201.

14 Geerhardus Vos, *Biblical Theology* (Grand Rapids, 1948), 143-182.

15 Ridderbos, *op. cit.*, 89.

16 *ibid.*

17 *idem.*, "The Inspiration and Authority of Holy Scripture," in ed., Donald K. McKim, *The Authoritative Word* (Grand Rapids, 1983), 187, 189.

18 Norman Shepherd, "The Nature of Biblical Authority," unpublished manuscript, 5, 7.

19 Andrew Sandlin, "The Word of the Sovereign is the True Battle for the Bible," in ed., Sandlin, *Keeping Our Sacred Trust* (Vallecito, CA, 1999), 10-25.

[20] Clark Pinnock is right to distinguish two conservative approaches relating to the issue of authority in Christianity. He takes as ideal types Cornelius Van Til and Carl F. H. Henry, in Pinnock's *Tracking the Maze* (San Francisco, 1990), 43-48. Henry follows his mentor Gordon Clark in rooting religious certainty in the infallible Scriptures, an "axiom of revelation." By contrast, Van Til is "authoritarian . . . right up front": he asks you to accept the Christian "system" as a presupposition for making sense of anything — including the Bible. In philosophical terms, this is "contextualism," while Henry's approach is "foundationalism." For Henry, you begin knowledge by presupposing an infallible Bible; for Van Til, the presupposition is the Triune God and His "system" — of which, to be sure, the infallible Bible is an indispensable part. For Van Til, certainty of Biblical infallibility does not rest on the consistency of its message, as it does for Henry; it rests on the assumption that the God Whom we presuppose could speak in no other way than infallibly. Biblical infallibility is not an "axiom" detached from the Christian "system" in which infallibility operates.

Appendix 3
The Errancy of the "Inerrancy of the Original Autographs" Theory

The Inerrant Autographs Versus the Infallible Apographs

One of the great theological myths of our times is that fidelity to the Sacred Scriptures as the unerring Word of God cannot be maintained apart from belief in "the inerrancy of the original autographs."[1] This is a relatively novel view in the history of the church, but it is certainly pervasive among today's evangelicals and fundamentalists. It has been a feature of the fundamentalist view of the Bible since almost the beginning of the fundamentalist movement. In the classic early work of fundamentalism titled, appropriately enough, *The Fundamentals*, James M. Gray, dean of Moody Bible Institute, wrote:

> [T]he record for whose inspiration we contend is the original record — the autographs or parchments of Moses, David, Daniel, Matthew, Paul or Peter, as the case may be, and not any particular translation or translations of them whatever. There is no translation absolutely without error, nor could there be, considering the infirmities of human copyists, unless God were pleased to perform a perpetual miracle to secure it [*i. e.*, the inspiration of the original-language copies].[2]

"Inerrancy," he goes on to say, is limited to the "parchment no living being has ever seen [*i. e.*, the original autographs]."

This view, shared by the overwhelming majority of modern conservatives of almost any theological persuasion, represents a decisive break with the Reformation view of the Bible. The Reformers, and particularly their immediate heirs, the so-called Reformed scholastics, would have found this idea stunning and suicidal.[3] They were little concerned with the autographs, but greatly concerned with the *apographs*, the extant original-language texts faithfully *preserved* within the bosom of the Faith and the church. *These* were the *locus* of Biblical authority. *These* (warts and all) constituted the infallible Word of God:

> By "original" and "authentic" text, the Protestant orthodox do not mean the *autographa* which no one can possess but the *apographa* in the original tongue which are the source of all versions. The Jews throughout history and the church in the time of Christ regarded the Hebrew of the Old Testament as authentic and for nearly six centuries after Christ, the Greek of the New Testament was viewed as authentic without dispute. It is important to note that the Reformed orthodox insistence on the identification of the Hebrew and Greek texts as alone authentic does not demand direct reference to *autographa* in those languages: the "original and authentic text" of Scripture means, beyond the autograph copies, the legitimate tradition of Hebrew and Greek *apographa*. The case for Scripture as an infallible rule of faith and practice and the separate arguments for a received text free from major (non-scribal) error rests on an examination of the *apographa* and does not seek the infinite regress of the lost *autographa* as a prop for textual infallibility.... [In related footnote 165 Muller observes: "A rather sharp contrast must be drawn, therefore, between the Protestant orthodox arguments concerning the *autographa* and the views of Archibald Alexander Hodge and Benjamin Breckinridge Warfield."][4]

The Westminster Confession of Faith, the great doctrinal symbol of the English-speaking Calvinists, did not argue for the inerrancy of the lost original autographs, but for the infallibility of the extant *apographs*:

> The Old Testament in Hebrew ... and the New Testament in Greek ... being immediately inspired by God, and **by his singular care and providence kept**

> **pure in all ages**, are therefore authentical; so as in all controversies of religion, the Church is finally to appeal unto them [*i. e.*, the apographs].[5]

Plainly, the *locus* of revelational authority is not the *autographa*, but the *apographa*. The Reformed stressed not merely the inspiration and infallibility, but also the *providential preservation*, of the Holy Scriptures. It is those providentially preserved Scriptures that are "authentical" and constitute the final court of theological appeal. In the same vein, the framers of the Formula Consensus Helvetica (1675), Calvinists from Geneva, confessed:

> ... the Hebrew Original of the Old Testament, **which we have received and to this day do retain** as handed down by the Jewish Church, unto whom formerly "were committed the oracles of God" (Rom. iii. 2), is, not only in its consonants, but in its vowels—either the vowel points themselves, or at least the power of the points — not only in its matter, but in its words, inspired of God, thus forming, together with the Original [apographs] of the New Testament, the sole and complete rule of our faith and life ....[6]

It has become fashionable for conservatives to snicker at and apologize for these Calvinists' suggestion that the Hebrew vowel points may have been divinely inspired, but one can never deny the high esteem in which they held the *preserved* — not principally the autographic — Word of God.

Likewise, Reformed dogmatician Francis Turretin (1623-1687), one of Calvin's and Beza's successors in the theological chair of Geneva and a framer of the Formula Consensus Helvetica cited above, posited the present original-language texts preserved in the church as the "original texts":

> By the original texts, **we do not mean the autographs** written by the hand of Moses, of the prophets and the apostles, which certainly do not now exist. We mean their apographs which are so called be-

> cause they set forth to us the word of God in the very words of those who wrote under the immediate inspiration of the Holy Spirit.[7]

In the nineteenth century, this providentially preserved Bible came under attack for conflicting with "the assured results" of modern science.[8] This involved everything from differences between accounts in the gospel records, to supposed errors in Old Testament genealogies, to alleged misquotations of the Old Testament by the New Testament, and so forth. Alan Richardson relates:

> At the end of the eighteenth century, as throughout it, the traditional conception of divine revelation was still everywhere accepted in western Christendom: Catholics and Protestants alike conceived of revelation as contained in inerrant propositions written down in the Bible by authors who were directly inspired by the Spirit of God. By the end of the nineteenth century this traditional view was no longer possible for those who had accepted the implications of what we have called the revolution in the historical method.[9]

One prime aspect of this historical method was textual criticism — the attempt to reconstruct the exact wording of ancient texts. For the most part, prior to the eighteenth century the church (both East and West) believed that textual transmission was the responsibility of the people of God in the church.[10] Variant readings, for example, were gauged according to their relation to Christian orthodoxy, the Faith itself; this, in large part, was the church's "textual criticism." With the advent of the Enlightenment practice of textual criticism, all of that changed. The Bible was to be treated as any other book.[11] The Enlightenment had a strong anti-supernaturalistic bias. Its scholarly methods reflected that bias. In the case of textual criticism, this means that the church could not take into account the supernatural, providential preservation of the Word of God. The same methods used to restore the original text of Shakespeare and Milton were used to restore the original texts of the Sacred Scriptures.

The fact that Shakespeare and Milton drafted qualitatively different writings from the Word of God made no difference.

Ancient Manuscripts and Apologetic Retreat

About the same time, several ancient New Testament manuscripts were discovered — so ancient that they predated most of the manuscripts available at the time. In significant places and in significant ways, these older, but more recently discovered, manuscripts differed from the reading of the vast majority of New Testament manuscripts used by the church for over a thousand years.[12] Because the leading objective of textual critics was to restore the original autographs of the Bible, these discoveries were hailed widely. It was widely assumed, for example, that the *oldest* texts are likely the more *accurate* texts, though a little thinking shows this to be false. If our goal is to restore the wording of the original writing, what is most important is not the antiquity of the manuscript, but the antiquity of the *reading* of the manuscript. The oldest manuscripts, in other words, do not necessarily preserve the oldest reading. In the Enlightenment climate of the time, though (and early evangelicals in particular were heavily influenced by the Enlightenment[13]), the discovery of these ancient manuscripts and the discipline of textual criticism in general were considered a great blessing by many Bible-believing Christians. Why? Because they were in the middle of a battle with skeptics and agnostics who claimed to have found serious errors in the Bible. With the advent of this Enlightenment textual criticism, conservatives who held to a high view of the Bible's authority could always argue, as fundamentalist-evangelicals do today, "Well, yes, there are many errors and mistakes in our present Hebrew and Greek texts and in our translations, but we can be certain that there were no errors and mistakes in the original autographs. In order to prove that the Bible is not the infallible Word of God, we would need to examine the original autographs; and since we cannot examine them, we have every reason to presume that they are inerrant."[14] This well-intended reasoning fails on several counts.

Fallibility Does Not Verify Infallibility

We learn the idea of Biblical infallibility from the Bible itself. If our present Bibles are somewhat unreliable and thus not the *locus* of infallibility, on what basis can we trust their teaching when it relates to infallibility? Conservatives often scoff at this argument. They claim that since the teaching of Biblical infallibility is so widely attested in the Bible, even if the passage that teaches it is not quite accurate in a single place, it is certainly accurate in others. If by this they mean that the doctrine of the Bible's infallibility is found in the overwhelming majority of Biblical manuscripts, the argument would have merit. But they cannot afford to make this argument, since for them the *locus* of infallible authority is not any single text or textual tradition like the *textus receptus*, but the original autographs themselves. If the original autographs are the infallible standard, and if we do not possess the original autographs or a replica of them, we can scarcely argue that we today can be infallibly certain that the Bible teaches its own infallibility. Infallibility is difficult to verify by means of fallibility.

Compromise With Covenant-Breakers

An additional error in adopting the "inerrancy of the original autographs" theory is that it surrenders to covenant-breaking unbelievers the grounds on which Biblical infallibility and textual transmission are to be argued. The so-called "neutral" or "eclectic" theories of textual criticism contend that any individual with sufficient training in textual studies can successfully engage in textual criticism — apart from his theological pre-commitments. In fact, a leading evangelical, F. F. Bruce, has argued it is *preferable* for textual critics to undertake their task *apart* from any dogmatic commitment.[15] His point is that if they possess theological pre-commitments, those commitments will likely influence their choices among variant readings. This is a naiveté of monstrous proportions — as though theological pre-commitments were avoidable! Men come to the Bible with either covenant-keeping or covenant-breaking presuppositions. Unbelievers (and other theological deviants) do not approach the Bible in the same manner as covenant-keeping Christians do.[16] How they approach the Bible will certainly influence how they practice textual criticism, just as it influences how they interpret the Bible. To suggest that textual criticism is a "neutral," "scientific" enterprise implies that unbelievers and other theological deviants have no "ax to grind" in their textual work — that they are committed to laying aside their God-hating presuppositions when plying their trade. Few assumptions could be more misguided.

Scripture and Orthodoxy

This is one reason that textual transmission traditionally has operated within the orthodox Faith and the church. Bart Ehrman has argued that the patristic church "corrupted" the text of Scripture by trying to make it conform to certain orthodox doctrinal pre-commitments, particularly in the area of Christology.[17] What he calls "corruption," of course, is often what orthodox Christians would simply refer to as God's providential preservation. God has preserved the correct reading of the text by means of His church — surely not a single sector of the church, much less a single denomination, but the entire orthodox church throughout history. To hold that textual criticism does not affect interpretation and doctrine is naive. "[T]extual criticism," Fee observes after discussing the doctrinal significance of variant readings, "rather than being simply an exercise for the expert preceding exegesis, is also an integral part of the interpretation of the Word of God."[18] If this is the case, and if unbelievers or heretics (learned though they may be) suppress God's truth revealed to them (*Rom. 1:18f.*), why should we expect that they would surrender this depraved suppression when they practice textual criticism? The proper province of textual transmission is the orthodox church, not the "scientific" academy.

Refreshing Liberal Honesty

It is surely odd that the same conservatives so quick to retreat to the autographs in order to defend inerrancy, so vociferously deny that any major doctrine is affected by textual variants[19] — especially when liberals have been much more honest than conservatives in recognizing that textual variation as addressed by modern textual criticism potentially poses a hazard to the orthodox view of the Bible. Evangelical-turned-liberal James Barr notes:

> Short of ignoring textual study altogether, or of taking the desperate step of affirming that the manuscripts of some particular tradition, for instance, those used in the text translated by the Authorized Version, were the bearers of unique divine inspiration [this is precisely the "desperate step," following my Reformed forebears, that I have taken — PAS], there was nothing for [fundamentalism] to do but to accept the validity of textual criticism and say that the inspiration attached to the original autographs, lost though they are.... In the vast majority of instances, where conservative interpreters appeal to the possibility of a corrupt text [as a defense against skeptics' charges against the Bible's infallibility], there is in fact no evidence at all that the text is corrupt [*i. e.*, the extant text does in fact preserve the original wording] .... [I]t is an attempt to get rid of a discrepancy by wishful thinking.[20]

Barr is quite wrong to suggest that the Bible is fallible, but quite right to chide conservatives for retreating to the original autographs in an attempt to bolster their view of Biblical infallibility in the face of skeptics' criticisms.

At this point, conservatives' apologetic gymnastics can become almost amusing. Douglas Stuart, for instance, in one breath cautions, "When two texts disagree, it is often difficult or even impossible to make a decision as to which of the two might in fact more closely represent the original autograph,"[21] and in the next breath reassures his readers,

"Evangelicals are free to admit weaknesses in the current copies of the Bible that are in their possession, while enthusiastically and confidently proclaiming the inerrancy or entire trustworthiness of the faith once for all delivered in the text of Scripture."[22] In other words, we cannot be sure of the wording of the text of the original writings, but we can be sure that this wording is inerrant — and we can be sure of this on the basis of our present errant texts!

If we say that modern textual criticism will only confirm and never refute Biblical infallibility and that no major doctrine is affected by the textual variants, we are only deluding ourselves. Textual criticism is not a neutral science (nor is any science, for that matter). Orthodox presuppositions shape an orthodox text; heterodox presuppositions shape a heterodox text. The doctrine of the providential preservation of the Bible holds that God Himself has superintended the transmission of the true Biblical text within the company of orthodox believers. In other words, *we cannot separate orthodox doctrine from textual transmission.* God preserves the true text no less than He preserves true doctrine, and He preserves true doctrine *by means* of preserving the true text.

The Theological Compromise of the "Inerrancy of the Autographs"

Conservatives have been petrified by the skeptics' accusation that the Bible is riddled with errors in that it conflicts not only with itself (internal contradictions), but also with the "assured results" of science, archeology, historical investigation, and the like (external contradictions). Rather than disputing the very ground from which the skeptics launch this charge, conservatives routinely retreat back into the supposed safe haven of the "inerrancy in the original autographs" theory. This retreat is not only tactically unwise; *it is ultimately subversive of the Faith.* As the inscripturated Word of God, the Bible is infallible. It is infallible because the God Whom the Bible reveals can speak in no other way than infallibly (*Jn. 17:17; Titus 1:2*). The doctrine of a Biblical infallibly is not an inductive postulate — in other words, we do not approach the Scripture to see *whether* the Bible does, in fact, claim its own infallibility.[23] Rather, the redeemed man, as a submissive creature to his Creator, knows that the Triune God is infallible by His very nature:

> It is not the content of the [Biblical] message that constitutes the message as authoritative; but rather it is the source, the author of Scripture, which is the authority[-]imparting factor.... The message may serve to arouse interest but it could not command obedience. It is God who speaks and faith is faith in God and his word. His word is authoritative because it is *his* word.... Infallibility is not something we ascribe to Scripture because we can put all of the pieces together but rather because God is its author.[24]

The question of Biblical infallibility rests ultimately in the character of God. Thus the argument for Biblical infallibility (like all ultimate claims) is necessarily circular: we affirm Biblical infallibility because the God Whom the Bible reveals could speak in no other way than infallibly, and because the Bible in which God is revealed asserts that God alone speaks infallibly.

Men deny Biblical infallibility not for intellectual reasons, but for ethical reasons — *they are at war with God*. Unbelieving covenant-breakers do not deny Biblical infallibility because it is hard to reconcile with "reason" or with the discoveries of the modern world — they deny Biblical infallibility because they are rebels.

Likewise, covenant-keeping Christians do not affirm Biblical infallibility because they can demonstrate that the Bible conforms to the canons of modern science in every detail — rather, they affirm Biblical infallibility because the God of the universe speaks in no other way than infallibly. In this vein, Rushdoony asserts:

> God's every word and act is infallible, not because it meets some standard of accuracy and truth and passes that test, but because God's word is the ultimate word, and there is nothing beyond God whereby we can judge, test, or prove God's word.[25]

This deeply reverential approach to the Bible was expressed most movingly by the great Dutch Calvinist Abraham Kuyper, whose sentiments warrant extensive citation:

> ... [I]t must be insisted that the Scripture as a whole, as finally presented to the Church, as to content, selection, and arrangement of documents, structure, and even words, owes its existence to the Holy Spirit, *i. e.*, that the men employed in this work were consciously or unconsciously so controlled and directed by the Spirit, in all their thinking, selecting, sifting, choice of words, and writing, that their final product, delivered to posterity, possessed a perfect warrant of divine and absolute authority.
>
> That the Scriptures themselves present a number of objections and in many aspects do not make the impression of absolute inspiration does not militate against the other fact that all this spiritual labor was controlled and directed by the Holy Spirit. For the Scripture had to be constructed so as to leave room for the exercise of *faith*. It was not intended to be approved by the critical judgment and accepted on this ground. This would eliminate faith. Faith takes hold directly with the fulness of our personality. To have faith in the Word, Scripture must not grasp us in our *critical thought*, but in the life of the *soul*. To believe in the Scripture is an act of life of which thou, O lifeless man! art not capable, except the Quickener, the Holy Ghost enable thee.[26]

This view of Biblical authority and infallibility breathes a spirit of affection for and devotion to the written Word of God that all machinations of Hell, all high-sounding critical theories, all subtle queries about the infelicities of the extant text cannot shake. The Word is infallible because it is *God's* Word, and it is known to be infallible only by God's verification in the heart of true believers within the context of the church. It is not as individuals isolated from the covenant community of the church, but as members of that church, to whom the Holy Spirit verifies the infallibility of the Bible. This orthodox covenant community throughout history is the repository (though never the creator or sustainer) of the text of Scripture. It *knows* the Bible in its possession is the infallible Word of God, for the God Who has revealed Himself as the church's covenant God could speak in no other way than infallibly. This truth is verified by faith, not demonstration (*Heb. 11*).

Man's knowledge is temporal, tentative, frail, and fallible; therefore, his understanding of God's revelation is temporal, tentative, frail, and fallible. God's knowledge is eternal, immutable, concrete, and infallible; therefore, His revelation is eternal, immutable, concrete, and infallible. Measuring the accuracy of the Word of God by men's tentative, frail, modern standards, is like, in Van Til's language, trying to illuminate the sun by means of a candle. Standards of scientific accuracy are possible precisely because of the unchangeable infallibility of the God Whom the Bible infallibly reveals.

The apographs, the providentially preserved Greek and Hebrew texts transmitted within the orthodox church,[27] and specifically the so-called Received Text of the New Testament — despite what we as fallible humans perceive as problems — *is* the infallible Word of God. This is the text that underlay all sixteenth- and seventeenth-century Protestant translations — in English, for example, Tyndale's New Testament, the Geneva Bible, the Great Bible, and the Authorized King James Version. Almost all modern translations — particularly in English — have abandoned this textual basis. The only suitable translation of the Bible is one that accurately reflects the apographic text. A leading example in English is the King James Version.[28]

Covenant-keeping Christians are not interested in *restoring* the wording of the *original* text; rather, they are interested in *retaining* the wording of the *orthodox* text — *this* is the infallible Word of God.

To the queries, therefore, "But what about the small discrepancies within the textual tradition of the Received Text? Or What about the 'obvious corruptions' in this textual family," we reply, "If there is no available criterion by which to judge discrepancies and corruptions, it is illogical to assert that their supposed appearance in the Received Text undercuts its infallibility." In other words, it is the Received Text (and, of course, in a derivative sense, faithful translations from it) that is itself the infallible text of the Sacred Scripture. This is the text faithfully preserved in the church for many, many centuries; and it reflects the reading of the vast majority of extant manuscripts. By simple faith the covenant community posits infallibility of this text as it stands before us.

I once was discussing this point with one of the leading conservative proponents of the "inerrancy of the original autographs" theory. He scoffed that the issue of the authority of the apographic text would do away with textual criticism, and everybody knows, he said, that textual criticism is essential to maintaining the Biblical text. His error was the supposition that "neutral," "scientific" textual criticism is the only valid form. The historically attested idea of a theological and creedal textual criticism rather than a "neutral," "scientific" textual criticism was simply not on his theological radar screen. But it is in fact the only reverent method of textual criticism. This, to be sure, is a completely different way of thinking from that to which modern conservatives are accustomed. By and large, they are not interested in maintaining the historic, Biblical view of Scripture, but in answering the latest charges by God-hating skeptics. They have never learned the lesson that *we do not frame our view of Biblical authority in terms of apologetics*. Our view of Biblical authority derives from our view of the nature of God Himself.

Infallibility and Immediacy

But perhaps the greatest error of all attaching to the "inerrancy in the original autographs" theory is that it pushes the infallible Word of God out of the reach of man and his concrete, immediate, historical circumstances. It is not the text in front of modern man that confronts him as the infallible Word of God. Rather, as he gains theological sophistication, the present text (whether the apographs or a faithful translation) becomes merely a shell or a shadow of God's infallible Word, which *really* resides in the mythical original autographs. This is to undercut the Bible's own teaching about itself. For example, in 2 Timothy 3:15-17, the *locus classicus* of the orthodox doctrine of the Bible's inspiration, we learn that the inspired Scriptures which profit the man of God are the Scriptures that Timothy knew "as a child." This refers to the preserved Old Testament and certainly not the Old Testament original autographs. In fact, there is every reason to believe the Old Testament with which Timothy was acquainted was the *Greek* translation of the Old Testament, the Septuagint. The point is not that translations should take precedence over the apographic (Greek and Hebrew) texts; rather, it is that the inscripturated Word of God to which man is to submit himself is not a mythical autographic text, but the providentially preserved text that stands before him. This recognizes the *immediacy* of God's inspired Word. "The word," declares St. Paul in citing Deuteronomy 30:14, "is nigh [near] thee, even in thy mouth, and in thy heart" (*Rom. 10:8*). The full citation in Deuteronomy reflects the immediacy of the Word; the Word is given immediately to man so that he may submit to and obey it:

> For this commandment which I command thee this day, it is not hidden from thee, neither is it far off. It is not in heaven, that thou shouldest say, Who shall go up for us to heaven, and bring it unto us, that we may hear it, and do it? Neither is it beyond the sea, that thou shouldest say, Who shall go over the sea for us, and bring it unto us, that we may hear it, and do it? But the word is very nigh unto thee, in thy mouth, and in thy heart, that thou mayest do it. See, I have set before thee this day life and good, and death and evil.... (*Dt. 30:11-15*)

The Word of God is alive and powerful, sharper than any two-edged sword (*Heb. 4:12*). The infallible Word is not the word limited to the past, an abstract word that exists only in the minds of conservative textual scholars frightened by the assaults of God-hating skeptics. The infallible Word of God is the immediate Word that stands before us. Its claims on our life are the claims of our Sovereign. Our response to that Word must be obedience, not skepticism.

---

[1] Greg L. Bahnsen, "The Inerrancy of the Autographa," in ed., Norman L. Geisler, *Inerrancy* (Grand Rapids, 1980), 151-193, and Benjamin Breckinridge Warfield, "The Inerrancy of the Original Autographs," in ed., Mark A. Noll, *The Princeton Theology, 1812-1921* (Phillipsburg, NJ, 1983), 268-274.

[2] James M. Gray, "The Inspiration of the Bible — Definition, Extent and Proof," in eds., R. A. Torrey, A. C. Dixon, *et al., The Fundamentals* (Grand Rapids [1917], 1980), 12.

[3] Theodore P. Letis, "The Protestant Dogmaticians and the Late Princeton School on the Status of the Sacred Apographa," *The Scottish Bulletin of Evangelical Theology*, Vol. 8, No. 1 [Spring, 1990], 16-42.

[4] Richard A. Muller, *Post-Reformation Reformed Dogmatics* (Grand Rapids, 1993), 433.

[5] *Westminster Confession of Faith* (Glasgow [1646], 1976), 23 [ch. 1, sec. 8], emphasis supplied.

[6] A. A. Hodge, *Outlines of Theology* (London, 1886), 656, 657, emphasis supplied.

[7] Francis Turretin, *Institutes of Elenctic Theology*, trans. George Musgrave Giger (Phillipsburg, NJ, 1992), 1:106, emphasis supplied.

[8] W. Neil, "The Criticism and Theological Use of the Bible, 1700-1950," in ed., S. L. Greenslade, *The Cambridge History of the Bible* (Cambridge, England, 1963), 3:238-293.

[9] Alan Richardson, "The Rise of Modern Biblical Scholarship and Recent Discussion of the Authority of the Bible," *ibid.*, 3:298.

[10] Edward F. Hills, *Believing Bible Study* (Des Moines, IA, 1967), ch. 2 and *passim*.

[11] Neil, *op. cit.*, 3:270.

[12] Gordon D. Fee, "The Textual Criticism of the New Testament," in ed., Frank E. Gaebelein, *The Expositor's Commentary on the Bible* (Grand Rapids, 1979), 1:427.

[13] D. W. Bebbington, "Evangelical Christianity and the Enlightenment," *Crux*, Vol. 25, No. 4 [December, 1989], 29-36.

[14] See, *e. g.*, Carl F. H. Henry, *God, Revelation and Authority* (Waco, TX, 1979), 4:207-209.

[15] F. F. B[ruce], "The Critical Study of Biblical Literature: Exegesis and Hermeneutics," in ed., Philip W. Goetz, *Encyclopedia Britannica* (Chicago,1988, 15th edition),14:851.

[16] Cornelius Van Til, *A Christian Theory of Knowledge* (Phillipsburg, NJ, 1969), ch. 3.

[17] Bart D. Ehrman, *The Orthodox Corruption of Scripture* (New York, 1993).

[18] Fee, *op. cit.*, 1:432.

[19] Stewart Custer, *The Truth About the King James Version Controversy* (Greenville, SC, 1981), 6.

[20] James Barr, *Fundamentalism* (Philadelphia, 1978 edition), 282-283. See also his *Beyond Fundamentalism* (Philadelphia, 1984), ch. 15.

[21] Douglas Stuart, "Inerrancy and Textual Criticism," in eds., Roger R. Nicole and J. Ramsey Michaels, *Inerrancy and Common Sense* (Grand Rapids, 1980), 102.

[22] *ibid.*, 117.

[23] Contra Clark Pinnock, *Biblical Revelation* (Chicago, 1971), 16.

[24] Norman Shepherd, "The Nature of Biblical Authority," unpublished manuscript, 7, 5, emphasis in original.

[25] Rousas John Rushdoony, *Systematic Theology* (Vallecito, CA, 1994), 1:29.

[26] Abraham Kuyper, *The Work of the Holy Spirit* (Grand Rapids [1900], 1946), 78, emphasis in original.

[27] Theodore P. Letis, *The Ecclesiastical Text* (Philadelphia, 1997).

[28] Edward F. Hills, *The King James Version Defended!* (Des Moines, IA, 1993 edition).